THE
Gilding
BOOK

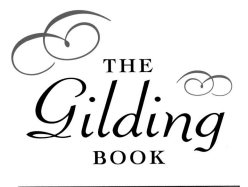

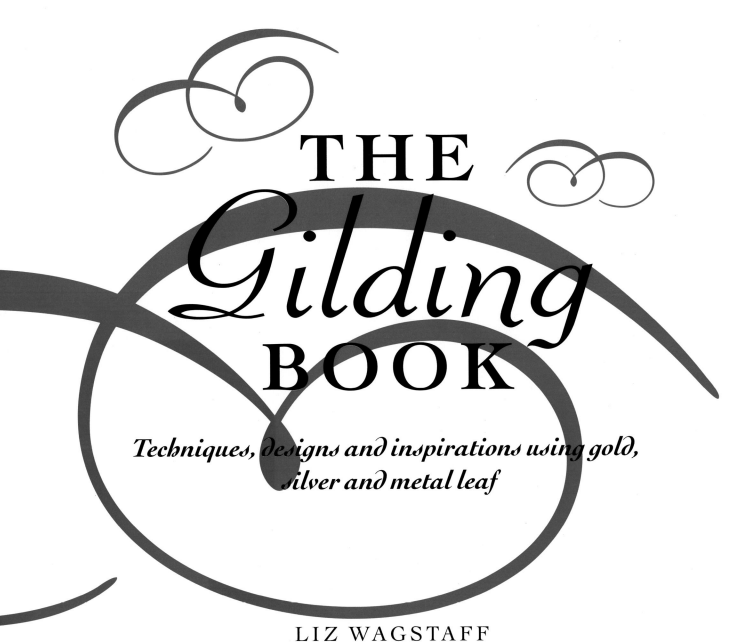

THE
Gilding
BOOK

Techniques, designs and inspirations using gold, silver and metal leaf

LIZ WAGSTAFF

Photographs by DEBBIE PATTERSON

LORENZ BOOKS
NEW YORK • LONDON • SYDNEY • BATH

This edition published in 1996 by Lorenz Books, an imprint of
Anness Publishing Limted
Administration office: 27 West 20th Street, New York, NY 10011

Lorenz Books are available for bulk purchase for sales promotion and premium use.
For details write or call the manager of special sales, Lorenz Books, 27 West 20th
Street, New York, NY 10011: (212) 807-6739

ISBN 1 85967 255 8

Publisher: JOANNA LORENZ
Senior Editor: LINDSAY PORTER
Designer: LISA TAI
Photographer and Stylist: DEBBIE PATTERSON
Step Photographer: LUCY TIZARD

Printed and bound in Hong Kong

CONTENTS

INTRODUCTION

Gilding is an ancient technique with an illustrious pedigree. Despite the advent of alternative metallic finishes, the traditional method is still used by many designers and craftspeople today.

THE GILDER'S ART

Gilding using real gold leaf has been a popular form of embellishment and decoration for many centuries. It was first introduced by the ancient Egyptians and many examples of their beautiful work can be seen in museums worldwide. Because of the high cost of gold, many less expensive metals have been developed in leaf form as substitutes for gilding.

The traditional techniques take time and care to master, but they are well worth the patience and dexterity required to produce items of great beauty. The substitute metals and newer techniques, however, can be just as effective and, when applied well, give similarly attractive results.

Even with the steady rise in the cost of gold and the introduction of substitute leaf and powders, the popularity of real gold leaf has not waned. The main reason appears to be that much of the new leaf looks good immediately after application, but it can quickly lose its brilliance on exposure to the air, while real gold leaf does not tarnish and can be restored to its original beauty when it becomes dirty simply by washing.

Many forms of real gold leaf come in combination with substitute leaf, and bronze powders are also available. They all come in a wide range of colors and tones, so that many different finishes can be achieved. With the advances in technology, many wild and wonderful colors are readily available in craft shops, enabling the gilder to produce fantasy finishes quite easily.

Metallic leaf is produced by beating the base metal until the thinnest sheet possible is achieved. Gold is very malleable and can be beaten into extremely thin sheets. Other metals are not so easily influenced and give thicker sheets, which can be cut with scissors. Real gold leaf is so fine that it needs to be handled with great care and it requires special tools and materials. These have not changed for centuries, giving the art of gilding a charming, timeless quality.

The use of substitute leaf and powders makes the art more accessible, and it can be applied to transform all manner of objects. New paints and primers have widened the scope for the surfaces that can be gilded, since previously unsuitable objects can now be prepared to take the leaf.

New developments in leaf and powders, gold pastes and sprays have developed rapidly over the last few years. By applying some of the finishing techniques explained in this book, these less traditionally gilded items will sit quite happily among those decorated by more advanced processes. Experiment with different techniques on dried flowers and foliage, vases and candle holders to create a shimmering array in your home.

Right: Humble objects such as stones and flowerpots are transformed into objects of beauty with gilding.

THE HISTORY OF GILDING

The ancient Egyptians were the first to begin experimenting with real gold embellishment. Examples of gilding have been found in the tombs of the pharaohs, the oldest dating back farther than 3,000 years. Probably the most famous recognizable antiquity is the gilded mask of Tutankhamen's mummy.

Until the eighteenth century and the discovery of platinum, gold was the most precious of metals. The art of gilding was developed to apply layers of precious metals to cheaper materials, such as wood and plaster.

The Italians' use of gold leaf in the Middle Ages was one of the most beautiful, and the use of a deep red gesso base gave their gilding a richness of color seldom achieved elsewhere. Fine examples of this form of gilding can be seen on the intricate frames of medieval Italian religious paintings as

Above: This nineteenth-century French gilded cockerel is a fine example of the ornately decorative effects possible with gilding.

well as on the panels of triptychs used as altarpieces.

It was also the Italians in the late sixteenth century who produced a gold effect by applying a varnish tinted with yellow over silver or white metal leaf. This technique is still used in the work of fairground decorators, although the metal used today is more likely to be aluminum.

During the nineteenth century, a leaf made from an alloy of zinc and copper called Dutch metal was developed as a substitute for gold. It is still used today when a gold effect is required, but at a fraction of the cost of real gold leaf. It is not intended as a long-term decoration on items that will be exposed to extreme weathering, as it tends to deteriorate with time.

In Britain, gilding has been used as a form of decoration since the Stuart period. It appears in its most decorative

Above: Gilded chimney piece in the Long Gallery, Lancaster House, London, built in the early nineteenth century.

Right: The main hall of Igumnov Mansion, Moscow, built in the late nineteenth century.

form in baroque and rococo interiors and was at its most splendid in the homes of continental Europe. English taste was more modest and gilt furniture and decoration was considered ostentatious until the latter part of the seventeenth century.

At the beginning of the eighteenth century, gilding played an important part in the decoration of classical interiors. Columns, moldings and other architectural details were emphasized by gilding in different tones, depending on

Above: The gold and white ballroom of Kharitonenko Mansion, Moscow. Gold has been used to embellish all architectural details.

the color of bole or gesso used underneath the leaf.

Gilding was used by the more eminent English architects to decorate the ballrooms and state apartments of great houses. Chinoiserie, with its strong Asian influence, was a popular form of decoration in eighteenth-century Europe, and gilding was used in combination with

lacquer techniques to produce trays, screens and other decorative items.

Throughout the nineteenth and twentieth centuries, gilding continued to evolve to adapt to the different styles and trends in interior decoration.

The sumptuous finish of gilding can still be used to glittering effect in our modern age, whether in contemporary or traditional interiors.

CONTEMPORARY GILDING

Gilding can be easily adapted to suit modern interiors and ever-changing trends in design. The choice of surface and different methods of application can create an amazing variety of finishes, especially when gilding is used on surprising objects. Famous designers such as Christian Lacroix and Donna Karan enjoy playing with gilding in their homes and Christian Lacroix's extravagant jewelry and glitzy clothes reflect his love of gilding. Gilding is as fashionable today as it has ever been and it always adds a touch of glamour and style to a room. Mix gilding with contemporary furniture and objets d'art to produce a stunning new look.

Many interior decorators and designers promote the craft of gilding in

Above: Glass topped gilded table, by Lilli Curtiss. The clean simple lines of the design are the perfect foil for the gilded finish.

their creations, often choosing the most unusual objects to decorate in this way. Even stark modern interiors can be enhanced by the use of gilding. Designers have experimented with gilding on natural objects such as driftwood, shells and stones to fit in with a minimalist style.

At the other extreme, historical influences are still very much in evidence in contemporary gilding, and much of the work of modern designers has its roots in classical and gothic styles as featured in many of today's interior decoration magazines. The recent trend towards fun and kitschy, furniture and interiors has also enhanced the popularity of gilding, while the gothic revival has inspired many people to scour markets and junk shops for items in an ecclesiastical style to gild and adorn their homes.

The new colors available in substitute metals and metallic powders have provided great scope for experimentation. Copper and aluminum leaf can be

applied to modern furniture for a contemporary effect. Gilded furniture can also be mixed with modern upholstery and materials with stunning results. When combined with paint effects, simple aluminum leaf can be transformed to give the appearance of iron or lead. Rust, verdigris and other patination finishes are all easy to achieve, and they complement gilding in the modern home. New designers apply gilding to a wide variety of surfaces, including ceramics and papier mâché. It is not unusual to see a whole door or window frame gilded, as cheaper metals make decorating large areas with gilding a viable undertaking, and it is very difficult to tell the difference between these cheaper finishes and the more costly ones.

Above: Gilded chairs by Lilli Curtiss. These striking contemporary designs are based on the alchemical symbols for gold.

Above: Medieval mirror by Lynette Smart. The frame is fiberboard, decorated with Dutch metal leaf, and aged with acrylic paint.

Above: Steel lights by Catherine Purves. Gilded in gold and aluminum Dutch metal leaf, these pieces are decorated with male and female figures.

The craft of gilding has opened up a whole new world of ideas for interior designers, whether they choose a traditional, modern or futuristic effect. It is a pleasing thought that this age-old art first developed by the ancient Egyptians has retained its allure today, and is certain to continue to capture the artistic imagination well into the next century.

Right: Clocks by Mark Thurgood. The wooden star clocks are decorated in gold and silver leaf, and aged with acrylic color. The crown clock is made from chemically patinated copper and broken Dutch metal leaf.

BASIC TECHNIQUES

Once you have decided that you would like to gild an object, you need to choose the look you would like to achieve. Pure gold leaf will stand the test of time, but powders and pastes add instant dazzle.

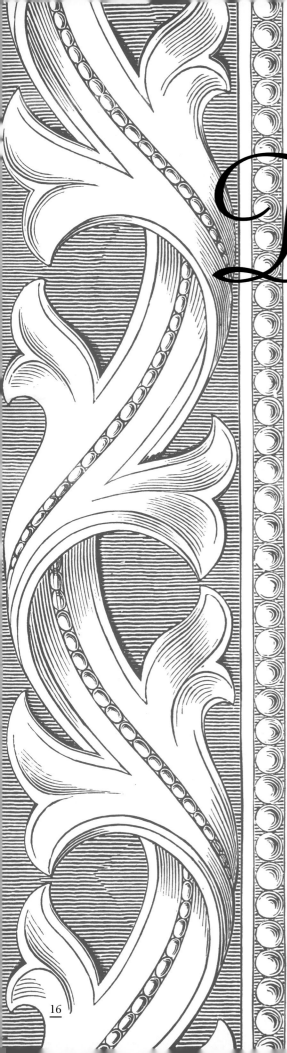

GILDING EFFECTS

The purity of gold leaf is measured in carats. The number of carats signifies the number of parts of pure gold in the metal, which is most commonly thought of as containing 24 parts. Pure gold contains 24 parts gold out of 24 and so is 24-carat gold. As other metals are added, the purity decreases, giving different colors of gold such as white, pale lemon and mid-green. Gold is also available in different weights and thicknesses. Apart from the differences in weight and color, gold leaf is supplied in two forms called loose and transfer. Loose-leaf comes in sheets between rouged paper. The pack or book of loose-leaf needs to be carefully handled, so that the leaves do not slide out. In the case of transfer leaf, a rectangle of tissue larger than the leaf is placed in each opening of the book and the book is then compressed so that the gold adheres to the tissue. Transfer leaf is the leaf most commonly used by amateur gilders. It was always considered a safer option by craftspeople working out of doors, as there was less chance of the precious metal disappearing in a gust of wind.

Transfer leaf is the only leaf suitable for oil gilding, but it is not available in such a wide range of weights and colors as loose-leaf. Although loose-leaf requires a larger initial outlay for equipment, it can be used on surfaces where it is difficult to apply transfer leaf. If you are planning to gild only one or two small items, transfer leaf may well be the cheaper option, but if you decide to start gilding on a regular basis, it is a good idea to master the skills of cutting and handling loose-leaf.

The cost of gold leaf varies greatly and often depends on where you buy it, the weight, the type of retailer and the country of origin. Some ordinary art suppliers stock gold leaf, but a wider selection will be available from gilding sundries suppliers or goldbeaters.

It does not always pay to use inferior gold. Experienced gilders can often achieve pleasing results using a cheaper leaf, but it is only due to their skill in handling the metal. Beginners should start with loose double-weight gold, which will withstand rougher treatment.

Silver and other metal leaf comes in slightly larger sheets than gold. Like gold, it is sold in books of twenty-five leaves. Because of the properties of other metals, they cannot be beaten as thinly as gold and have to be sealed and varnished once they have been laid. Silver or copper leaf can be sealed with a clear varnish to preserve its own appearance, or silver leaf can be sealed with a yellow varnish to produce the effect of gold. Silver leaf should be carefully wrapped when stored, to protect it from the air. The edges may need regular trimming to remove the dark lines that might be visible during laying.

From the Middle Ages to the eighteenth century, tin was a popular metal for its bright white, non-tarnishing finish. Today white gold, platinum, palladium and aluminum are more likely to be used instead. Platinum is very expensive and is

available in small sheets, as is palladium. Aluminum is much cheaper and is available in sheets approximately 6 inches square. It has a slightly grayish color. White gold can be beaten thinner than any of the other metals and gives the most brilliant surface.

Schlag leaf, more commonly known as Dutch metal, is quite a thick leaf made from a zinc and copper alloy and comes in 6-inch sheets. It is available in shades of copper, red and yellow. This leaf tarnishes quite easily and should be well varnished if required for more than a temporary finish. As this leaf is cheap, it is quite often used for theatrical props and sets. It can be bought in packs of 25 to 500 leaves and there is usually no interleaving tissue, so it should be well wrapped when stored.

Above: Dutch metal transfer leaf was used to add embellishment to plain wax candles.

Gold can also be bought ground up and mixed with a small amount of gum arabic and formed into small tablets. This form of gold is expensive and used mainly for restoration purposes. Gold in powder form was once used for japan work but is not now readily available.

Left: Empty coconut shells were gilded on the inside with Dutch metal transfer leaf, to create unusual holders for candles.

Whichever material you decide to use, buy the best quality you can afford from a reputable supplier who will be able to advise you on the correct materials and tools for your intended project.

Gold pastes, paints and sprays are also widely available. Although they don't produce quite the same effect as gilding and quickly lose their lustre, they are worth considering as a cheap alternative to gilding.

Whichever technique you choose, the surface to be gilded needs to be properly prepared so that the finish is pleasing and stays beautiful for a long time. For the best results, follow the preparation instructions in the techniques section for your chosen effect.

It is possible to make your own, but this is quite time-consuming and not really necessary given the wide range of other materials on the market. Bronze powders, on the other hand, are easy to obtain and come in several varieties and colors. They tarnish quite quickly, so they must be varnished. There are tarnish-resistant makes, but these are much more expensive. The colors range from pale gold to copper and antique bronze. Ordinary powdered bronzes usually have large flakes (though they're invisible to the naked eye), while lining bronzes are finer and burnishing bronzes are finer still.

If you want to produce a look similar to real gold leaf but in a third of the time and with little preparation, you could choose Dutch metal or another substitute metal. The beauty of the gold color then needs to be enhanced using shellac varnish but the results can be stunning. It is also possible to produce deceptively authentic-looking pieces using paint techniques and distressing.

If you choose real gold leaf, the proper tools and materials are essential – you cannot cut on the cost if you wish to achieve a perfect look. Using the incorrect tools and materials may not give you the results you had hoped for, and could turn out to be a very expensive mistake. Any leaf, whether real or substitute, will need fixing. This should be taken into consideration when you are choosing to gild an object that will either be kept outside or be exposed to wear and tear.

The size of the area to be gilded should also be taken into consideration when choosing materials. If you wish to cover a large object, the expense of using real gold leaf could be prohibitive, so it is worth considering a more cost-effective substitute leaf, which will give an equally pleasing result.

Pastes and powders are both readily available in a wide variety of colors and tones of gold, copper, bronze and silver. Liquid leaf is another good alternative when time and cost are important issues.

Above: Gilded mirror with candle sconces by Lilli Curtiss. The artist created an aged effect to complement the gothic-style design.

MATERIALS

Acrylic paints: Like oil paints, the more expensive the paint, the more intense and fast the colors. Dilute acrylic paints with water and mix them with latex paint for a variety of paint effects.

Bronze, aluminum and silver powders: These fine particles of metal can be mixed with varnish or blown or brushed on to size. They can be used to color design work, or on small objects with fine detail. They can be mixed with an ormoline medium for fabric painting.

Ceramic tile adhesive: Used for fixing tiles, mosaic pieces and other small objects to surfaces, this adhesive is available in a waterproof form for extra strength if required.

Edible leaf or warq: This real gold or silver leaf is made by hammering and flattening small balls of gold or silver into very thin sheets and is used to decorate Indian food for royal and religious ceremonies.

Eggshell paint: This oil-based paint should be applied on an oil-based undercoat. It gives a surface suitable for oil-based glazes and oil paints. Clean and dilute with paint thinner.

Filler: These come in various grades and are used to fill cracks or holes in wood and plaster. Filler dries to a hard, resilient surface, although it is not as smooth as putty.

French enamel varnish: This is available in many different tones and colors, the most common of which is amber. It can be used to seal and protect gilded items and to change or enhance the color. Spattering amber varnish onto distressed surfaces will add to the aged effect.

Gesso: This fine chalk powder is the key ingredient of gesso solution. White or colored ready-made acrylic gessos are also now available.

Gilding water: This liquid is made from water, methylated spirit and rabbit skin glue and is used in water gilding.

Gold leaf: Gold leaf is available as loose- or transfer leaf. Both types come in books of twenty-five leaves. Gold leaf is available in many tones, weights and thicknesses and is classed in carats.

Gold and silver paints: These are made in the same way as liquid leaf but from cheaper materials. They are useful for stenciling and for decorative painting.

Gold pastes: These are available in many forms and in tones of gold, silver and aluminum. They are often used in restoration work.

Graphite powder: When added to paints and varnishes, this powder gives a deep gray to black metallic effect.

Liquid leaf: This mixture of metallic powder and deep red primer can be used to cover a wide variety of surfaces. It comes in many shades.

Methylated spirit: This spirit is used to clean brushes after using polishes and some oil-based primers. It is also used to dilute gilding water and for distressing gilded surfaces.

Oil-based size or japan gold size: This size can be bought in various drying times. The longer the drying time, the shinier the gold will be when applied. This size is more resilient than water-based size.

Oil paints: There are many different types of oil paints. The more expensive they are, the more intense and fast the colors. Dilute oil paints with varnish, paint thinner or linseed (boiled) oil.

Paint thinner: This oil-based solvent is used to dilute oil-based paints and varnishes and to clean up after using oil-based paints.

Powder pigments: This ground pigment is used to mix paints and tint water- or oil-based paints, stains and varnishes. ➤

Rabbit skin glue: This comes in granule form and constitutes part of the mix for gesso and gilding water.

Red clay: This clay was traditionally handmade with rabbit skin glue and is now available ready-made to give a smooth surface for water gilding. It also comes in yellow, black and blue.

Red oxide metal primer: This primer is the ideal base coat for metal before applying paint or substitute leaf. It prevents rust and allows paint to take to the surface. It also comes in spray form. Metal primers are available in different colors to suit different purposes and specific metals.

Rottenstone: This stone-colored powder is used in the antiquing process and is usually applied to areas with a large amount of molding and detail.

Schlag or composition leaf (Dutch metal): This looks like gold leaf but is much cheaper and is made from a copper and zinc alloy. It is available in 6-inch square sheets.

Scumble glazes: Available in water-based and oil-based mixes, these glazes produce a translucent effect and lengthen the working time of the water- and oil-based paints widely used for decorative painting effects.

Shellac and polishes: Shellac and polishes come in many guises, such as button polish and transparent polish. They can be used to seal and protect gold but they will affect the color. Shellac is the ideal way of enhancing the hue of Dutch metal and other substitute leaf.

Silver, copper and aluminum leaf: These leaves are 6 inches square and come in books of twenty-five to five hundred loose- or transfer leaves.

Spray paints: Oil- and water-based spray paints come in a vast range of colors. There are different tones of gold spray paint, and silver and copper paints are also available.

Talc: Fine powdered talc is used in a pounce bag to cover a surface before sizing to make sure that the area is clean and that the leaf will adhere only to the sized areas.

Undercoat: Oil-based and quick-drying water-based undercoats are both available and provide a base coat for the appropriate top coat. The primer stabilizes the surface in preparation for paint.

Varnishes: Oil-based and water-based varnishes come in various finishes, ranging from matte to satin and gloss.

Water-based size: This fast-drying synthetic size sets tacky after 15 to 20 minutes. It can be used for oil gilding and with bronze powders and substitute leaf.

Waxes: Clear and colored waxes are both available and are used as sealants or to protect gilded objects. Colored waxes can be used to change the tone of a gilded object.

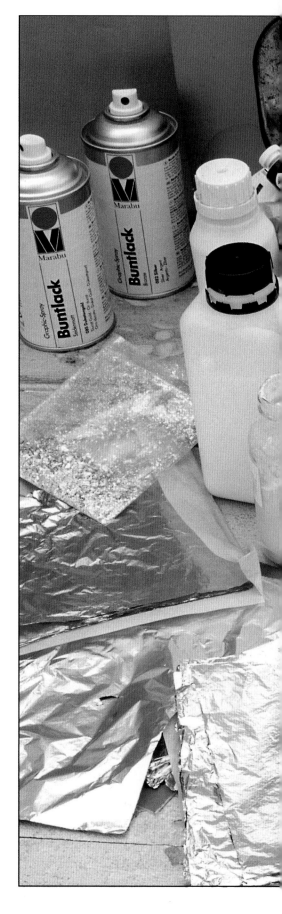

Right: The gilder's tools of the trade, including sizes, undercoats, gessos, and gold leaf and powders.

EQUIPMENT

Agate burnishers: These are made from a small piece of agate mounted in brass on a wooden handle and are available in various sizes and shapes. They are rubbed over water-gilded surfaces to obtain a high and brilliant shine.

Brushes: Different brushes will be needed for different purposes:

Badger brushes are very expensive. A cheaper and more environmentally friendly alternative is lily bristle. These brushes are used for softening glazes and varnishes. They should be cleaned and treated with care.

Bristle brushes are inexpensive and hard-wearing. They can be used for applying a wide range of paints, glazes and varnishes and are available in varying sizes and widths.

Gilder's tips are wide, soft brushes used to pick up real gold leaf before applying it to a surface.

Hog's-hair brushes are available in various shapes and sizes with flat or round heads for mixing and applying clay colors.

Household and *decorator's brushes* are used for applying paints, undercoats and some varnishes. It is useful to have a range of different sizes.

Sable brushes are quite costly but are invaluable for detailed painting and decoration.

Stencil brushes are short-haired, coarse-bristled brushes used for stencil designs.

Stippling brushes are expensive brushes made of pure bristle used for taking dust off glazes.

Sword liners are designed for painting decorative lines on furniture and for producing veins on marbling.

Cloths: Cotton rags are the best type of cloths for use in gilding and producing other decorative finishes. They can be bought in packs or made from old sheets. Cotton dusters are ideal for burnishing delicate surfaces.

Cotton balls: Use these for pressing real gold leaf into place and for small cleaning jobs.

Double boiler or bain marie: Use a double boiler for melting beeswax pellets, ready-made gessos and sizes. You could improvise your own double boiler by placing a saucepan over another one containing boiling water.

Drop cloths and newspaper: Use either to protect your room and work surface during gilding and painting projects.

Flower mister: Use this to spray water or methylated spirit onto surfaces to disperse oil-based or water-based glazes.

Gilder's knife: This special knife is used to cut loose-leaf.

Gilder's pad: This soft pad is surrounded by a screen of parchment or a similar paper screen to shield gold leaf from drafts.

Gloves: Heavy-duty household gloves are useful for stripping wood and for patination. Use disposable gloves for smaller decorative gilding jobs.

Glues: Epoxy resin glue, rubber-based glue and white glue are all useful in decorative work, and it is worth having a collection of different types.

Mask: Wear a mask when working with bronze powders, sprays and some oil-based glazes. Masks are also useful when working in confined areas with any oil-based products.

Masking tape: Use a low-tack type of tape for masking off areas and securing stencils.

Measuring tools, pens and pencils: These are necessary for positioning and measuring when stenciling and doing decorative painting.

Mutton cloth: Available in roll form, this cloth can be used for many decorative finishes and for cleaning up.

Natural sponge: Sea sponges are used to produce a variety of decorative finishes.

Paint kettles: Paint kettles are available in metal or plastic for mixing paints and glazes. Oil-based paints and glazes should not be stored in plastic.

Sandpaper: This abrasive paper comes in different grades for smoothing as well as producing an adhesive key for finishes. Wet-and-dry sandpaper is the best type for use on furniture and other items to be gilded.

Scalpels and craft knives: Collect various types of scalpel and craft knife for decorative work and for cutting stencils.

Steel or wire wool: This abrasive mix of metal fibers comes in different grades for smoothing and providing a key for finishes. It is also used for distressing gilded surfaces with methylated spirit.

Stencil card: You can use this special card of manila coated in boiled oil to make your own stencils.

Above: A selection of brushes for gilding, plus other essentials, such as a craft knife and gloves for small decorating jobs.

WATER GILDING

THE AGE-OLD TECHNIQUE OF WATER GILDING IS DIFFICULT TO MASTER, BUT THE RESULTS ARE TRULY MAGNIFICENT. THE

SECRET TO SUCCESSFUL RESULTS LIES IN THE PREPARATION OF THE SURFACE PRIOR TO GILDING. BOTH GOLD AND SILVER CAN

BE APPLIED USING THIS METHOD, FIXED WITH A SIMPLE GILDING WATER WHICH IS MADE BY ADDING A SMALL AMOUNT OF

METHYLATED SPIRIT TO WATER. THIS TECHNIQUE SHOULD BE CONFINED TO SMALL AREAS, AND IS NOT SUITABLE FOR LARGE

PIECES. GESSO IS USED TO PREPARE THE SURFACE BEFORE APPLICATION — IT GIVES A TOUGH, RESISTANT, YET PERFECTLY

SMOOTH SURFACE TO WORK ON. WOODEN FRAMES AND PLASTER DETAILS ARE IDEAL FIRST PROJECTS

1 Make sure that the surface you are gilding is clean and dry. Fill any cracks or holes with putty or filler and sand when dry. Melt rabbit skin glue granules in a bain marie. This will take approximately 5 to 10 minutes. When the granules are completely dissolved, the size will be the consistency of runny caramel. Sift just enough gesso powder into the melted granules to color the liquid. Heat over the bain marie until the liquid is translucent. Paint onto the surface so that it takes into the grain and leave the object to dry overnight.

2 Melt two parts rabbit skin glue to one part water. Take off the heat and sift in enough gesso to come above the liquid. Put back over the heat and stir well with a brush to dissolve all the lumps. While still warm, apply to the surface. Apply up to twelve coats. Each coat will take 10 to 15 minutes to dry. Try to complete this stage on the same day and leave the final coat to dry overnight. Alternatively, apply up to twelve coats of ready-made gesso in white or your chosen color.

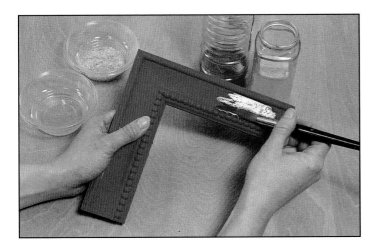

3 To make the gilding water, half-fill a jar with water. Slowly add methylated spirit until the water is lightly colored. Add a teaspoon of melted rabbit skin glue. Stir well until the solution is thoroughly mixed. Paint a small amount on to the area you wish to gild first. It will enable the leaf to adhere to the surface.

4 Gently place loose gold leaf on to the dampened surface and press down lightly with cotton balls. Continue painting on the gilding water and applying the gold leaf until the whole area is covered. Any small bare patches can be covered using a sable brush and small pieces of leaf. Leave to dry for 1 hour.

5 When the surface is dry, burnish with an agate burnisher, going over the surface several times until a deep shine begins to appear. Do not press too hard, since this will soften the gesso.

6 To distress the surface to give an aged effect, gently rub the surface with steel wool. Do not rub too hard and take care to distress only the areas that would receive wear naturally.

7 Seal the whole surface with clear wax. Leave to dry, and then polish with a soft cloth to improve the luster.

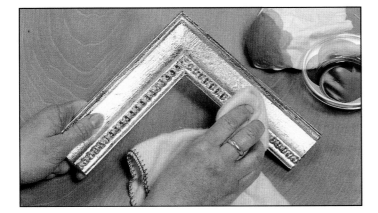

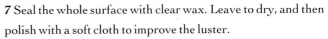

OIL GILDING

OIL GILDING CAN BE UNDERTAKEN ON OIL-BASED OR WATER-BASED PRIMERS AND BASE COATS, AS WELL AS ON

LACQUERED SURFACES. OMIT STEPS 1 AND 2 IF APPLYING OIL GILDING TO ANY OF THESE SURFACES. APPLY GESSO

(FOLLOWING STEPS 1 AND 2 OF THE WATER GILDING INSTRUCTIONS) IF YOU WISH TO ACHIEVE OPTIMAL RESULTS, SINCE

IT GIVES THE MOST PERFECT SURFACE FOR GILDING. YOU MAY WANT TO PAINT A PRIMER OR BASE COAT ONTO THE

GESSO PRIOR TO OIL GILDING

1 If you want to gild only a small area when undertaking a design on furniture, use talc to produce a clean, dust-free and greaseproof surface. The talc will prevent the leaf from adhering to unsized areas, thus ensuring perfect accuracy. Put the talc in a pounce bag and wipe over the surface to give an even layer. Wipe off any excess talc with a soft brush, making sure that the talc is well rubbed in before painting on the size.

2 At this stage, you can use either water-based or oil-based size. Water-based size dries more quickly, becoming clear and tacky after 20 minutes. It can be tinted with watercolor for accurate application of the leaf. Apply a thin and even coat to the surface, avoiding air bubbles. Wash out the brushes with soap and water. Oil-based size comes in three types, which dry in 3, 12 or 24 hours. Drying times can be affected by atmosphere and climate, but follow the instructions on the bottle. Oil-based size can be tinted with oil colors to produce a base tint. Apply a thin and even coat to the surface.

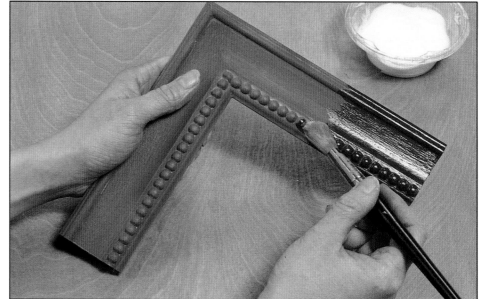

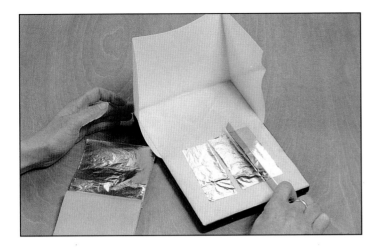

3 Use loose- or transfer leaf. Open the book of leaf over a gilder's pad and blow the leaf onto the pad. You can cut the leaf into smaller pieces with a gilder's knife if required. Pick up some leaf with the knife and put it on the pad. Gently blow the leaf to make sure it is flat. Cut the leaf by drawing the blade towards you once.

4 To help in picking up the leaf, spread a little petroleum jelly on your forearm and brush the gilder's tip over the jelly. Apply more jelly at frequent intervals. Using the tip, remove the leaf from the pad. Transfer leaf is applied with a short-bristled brush or your thumb by pressing down firmly after the leaf is held on to the size.

5 Lay the leaf onto the sized area using the tip. Each sheet of gold should overlap the next. Brush over with cotton balls.

6 Any loose pieces or skewings can be brushed away with a soft brush and should be saved to be reused later.

7 Make sure the area is free of any loose gold, and seal with a wax or polish. Rub the polish onto the gilded area with a brush or by making a polishing rubber. Cover some batting with a clean rag, leaving an opening at the top. Add a few drops of polish to soak the batting. Close up the rag and when the liquid soaks through, start rubbing the gilded surface. The surface can be buffed up with a soft cloth when dry. Oil gilding can also be distressed using wire wool, fine sandpaper or a rag with a little paint thinner. Always be careful when distressing and don't rub too hard.

ALTERNATIVE METHODS

THERE IS A WIDE RANGE OF MATERIALS THAT GIVE THE APPEARANCE OF GILDING, AT A FRACTION OF THE PRICE AVAILABLE NOW.

LIQUID LEAF, GOLD POWDERS, PASTES AND SPRAYS ARE AVAILABLE FROM MOST GOOD ART SUPPLIERS AND FRAMING SHOPS, AND

COME IN A WIDE RANGE OF METALLIC HUES, FROM SILVER THROUGH TO ALL SHADES OF GOLD, COPPER AND BRONZE. LIQUID LEAF

IS FAST DRYING AND EASY TO USE, WHILE GOLD SPRAYS SHOULD FORM A STAPLE OF ANY

SUPPLY CABINET. FRENCH ENAMEL VARNISH CAN BE USED ON ALL THESE MATERIALS ◠

LIQUID LEAF

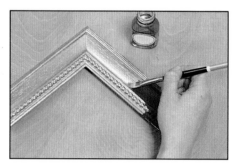

1 Apply an oil- or water-based primer to the surface to be gilded and let dry. Paint on a base coat in the desired color and leave to dry.

2 Shake the bottle of liquid leaf well and brush onto the surface with a real bristle brush or a gilding brush. Leave to dry, which usually takes about 20 minutes

depending on the brand. Seal with varnish. The manufacturer will usually recommend a sealant, but a polyurethane varnish or shellac will work.

PASTES

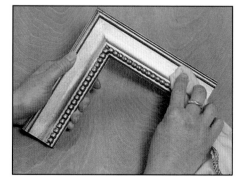

1 Apply an oil- or water-based primer to the surface to be gilded and leave to dry. Paint on a base coat in the desired color and leave to dry. The base color will enhance the final tone of the gold.

2 Apply the paste to the surface using a cloth or brush. Rub it in well, paying particular attention to any areas of detail. Leave to dry.

3 Rub the surface with a soft cloth, then seal with a wax or polish and polishing rubber if required.

POWDERS

1 Apply an oil- or water-based primer to the surface to be gilded and leave to dry. Paint on a base coat in the desired color and leave to dry. The base color will enhance the final tone of the gold. Apply oil- or water-based size and leave to become tacky.

2 Place a little powder at a time on a saucer and dip a brush into the powder, tapping off any excess, and brush it onto the size. Alternatively, lift the loaded brush over the surface and gently blow the powder on to the size, making sure that the whole area is covered. Always work in a well-ventilated area and a good distance from the powder. If covering a large surface, use the brush-on method and wear a mask.

3 Seal with a polishing rubber or a coat of French enamel varnish. The color of the varnish adds a jewel-like finish to the gold.

PAINTS AND SPRAYS

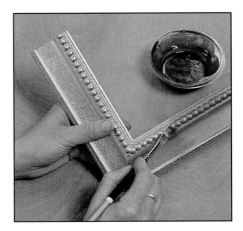

1 Apply an oil- or water-based primer to the surface and leave to dry. Paint or spray on a base coat in the desired color and leave to dry. The base color will enhance the final tone of the paint or spray.

2 Shake the paint can or spray can well. If painting, paint an even coat onto the surface and leave to dry. Repeat if necessary. If spraying, work in a well-ventilated area and hold the can 12 inches from the surface. Spray an even coat all over the surface. Leave to dry.

3 Spray or paint does not need to be varnished, but an amber shellac or colored French enamel varnish will enhance the color.

PREPARING SURFACES

PREPARING SURFACES FOR GILDING MUST BE DONE WELL IF THE END RESULT IS TO BE AS SUCCESSFUL

AS POSSIBLE. EACH TYPE OF SURFACE REQUIRES A DIFFERENT PREPARATION. IT IS NOT WORTH

SKIMPING ON THE PREPARATION STAGE WHEN WORKING WITH REAL GOLD LEAF, OR SOME OF THE

OTHER MORE COSTLY MATERIALS, SINCE THE RESULTS CAN BE VERY DISAPPOINTING AND EXPENSIVE

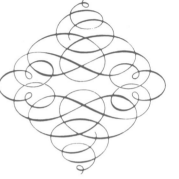

GLASS AND CERAMICS

1 Wash and dry the glass thoroughly. If you are gilding the whole surface, apply an acrylic primer and leave to dry. If you are gilding a smaller design, mark this on the glass and paint the area to be gilded with the primer.

2 Paint on a base coat of ceramic paint and leave to dry. Sand lightly with fine sandpaper and dust off before sizing. (If you are stenciling with gold paint, make sure the paint is suitable for glass.)

PLASTER

1 Make sure the surface is clean and dry. Seal with a coat of unibond and leave to dry. If the surface is old and flaky, apply a coat of stabilizing primer.

2 Apply gesso or acrylic primer as required.

METAL

1 If the metal is old, or in poor condition, remove any dirt or rust with steel wool or with wet-and-dry sandpaper.

2 Apply the appropriate metal primer (in this case red oxide metal primer). Leave to dry before applying another color if required.

STONE

1 Make sure the surface is clean and dry. Seal with a coat of unibond and leave to dry.

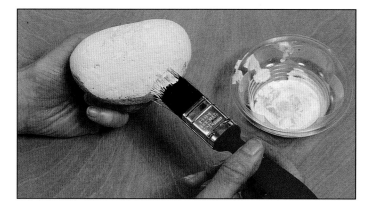

2 Apply acrylic primer. (It is not recommended to use real gold leaf on stone, so gesso is not required.)

PLASTIC

1 Wash and dry the plastic thoroughly. Fill any holes with car body repair filler. Sand with fine sandpaper and dust off.

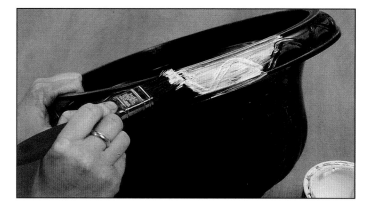

2 Apply one coat of stabilizing primer and leave to dry, then apply one coat of acrylic primer.

SPECIAL EFFECTS

THE PAINT FINISHES DESCRIBED IN THIS SECTION MAKE PERFECT BASES FOR MOST GILDING TECHNIQUES. PREPARE

ONE OF THE EFFECTS BELOW, THEN COMBINE WITH GILDING FOR STUNNING RESULTS. THE FOUR PAINT FINISHES

DESCRIBED ARE SHOWN IN THE TRADITIONAL COLORS, BUT TRY USING SOME MORE UNUSUAL ONES FOR

INTERESTING ALTERNATIVES

COLORWASH

1 Apply one coat of acrylic wood primer to the surface and leave to dry.

2 Apply one coat of white or tinted emulsion to the primed surface and leave to dry.

3 In a container, mix six parts acrylic scumble glaze with one part latex or acrylic paint. Mix well.

4 Dip a dry brush into the glaze and apply to the surface using random strokes and allowing some of the base color to show through. Leave to dry.

TORTOISESHELL

1 Apply one coat of acrylic wood primer and leave to dry. Apply one coat of vinyl emulsion in a bamboo shade, or spray gold.

2 Mix a little acrylic scumble glaze and water with three shades of acrylic artist's color: yellow-ochre, raw umber and burnt umber.

3 Using a separate brush for each color, dab the paint onto the surface in a diagonal direction. Gently skim over the surface with a softening brush to blend the colors into each other.

4 Using a bristle brush, randomly spatter some brown ink onto the surface to give the occasional spotting often seen on tortoiseshell. Leave to dry and seal with a varnishing wax or polish.

LACQUER

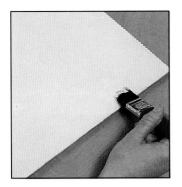

1 Apply a synthetic gesso to the surface and leave to dry. Apply four or five more coats of gesso, leaving each coat to dry before applying the next, and sanding down between each coat.

2 Dilute some shellac with a little methylated spirit and apply a single coat to the gesso. Leave to dry.

3 Apply a coat of lacquer or gloss paint and leave to dry overnight. Sand down with wet-and-dry sandpaper. Repeat this stage up to four times, sanding down after each coat of lacquer or gloss paint. The more coats applied, the better the finish and depth of color will be.

4 Apply a coat of polyurethane varnish tinted with oil color or a little lacquer or gloss. Leave to dry overnight.

LAPIS LAZULI

1 Apply an oil-based undercoat and leave to dry. Apply an ultramarine-tinted low-odor eggshell paint and leave to dry overnight.

2 Mix one part ultramarine oil color with two parts oil-based scumble glaze. Do the same with black oil color. Dilute with paint thinner to make the consistency of light cream. Apply these colors to the surface so that the ultramarine predominates with diagonal patches of black.

3 Gently skim over the surface with a softening brush to blend the colors into each other and eradicate the brush marks.

4 Before the paint dries, dilute white, yellow-ochre and black oil colors with paint thinner to make the consistency of light cream. Using a separate brush for each color, spatter over the wet surface in any order. Using a bristle brush, gently flick some bronze powder onto the surface to give the illusion of fool's gold. Leave to dry for 24 hours.

FINISHING OFF

IT IS IMPORTANT TO SEAL YOUR PIECE PROPERLY AFTER GILDING, AS THIS WILL ENSURE THE LONG LIFE OF THE

GILDING EFFECT. WHAT COULD BE MORE DISAPPOINTING THAN WATCHING YOUR LOVINGLY TRANSFORMED

ITEMS DISTRESS WITH AGE? FOLLOW THE GUIDELINES FOR EACH DIFFERENT TECHNIQUE AND MATERIAL TO

ENSURE THAT THE SEALANT YOU ARE USING IS RIGHT FOR THE JOB

POLISHING WITH SHELLAC

Using a brush or cloth, lightly cover the surface with the polish and leave to dry. Buff with a soft cloth.

USING A POLISHING RUBBER

Cover some batting with a clean rag, leaving an opening at the top. Add small drops of polish to soak the batting. Close up the rag and rub the gilded surface. Buff with a soft cloth when dry.

VARNISHING WITH AMBER SHELLAC

Using a soft varnishing brush, apply a thin, even coat of amber shellac to the surface and leave to dry. This method will improve the gold tone of Dutch metal.

VARNISHING WITH FRENCH ENAMEL

Using a soft varnishing brush, apply a thin, even coat of varnish to the surface. The different tones of French enamel varnish will enhance the look of substitute metallic effects.

DISTRESSING

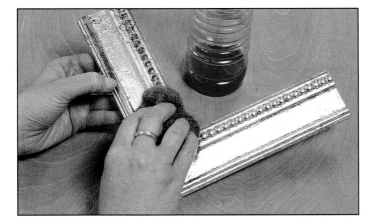

Gilding can be distressed before polishing or varnishing. Using steel wool on its own or dipped in a little methylated spirit, gently rub areas of detail or highlights. Take care to rub only those areas that would receive wear naturally, so that the distressing does not look false. Fine sandpaper can also be used.

SPATTERING

If you have distressed the gilding before sealing, a fine spattering of amber French enamel varnish may be used on areas of substitute leaf sealed with shellac or varnish. Use a stiff bristle brush and vary the size of dots by spattering from different distances from the surface.

RESTORING

Restoring items is a most rewarding activity. Antique restoration requires great skill and if an item is very old or valuable, it is advisable to take it to a professional. If the item has been gilded in real gold leaf, make sure you match the carat as closely as possible. A good gilding sundries supplier should be able to help.

Plaster

Either mold and cast any missing sections yourself using latex or get a plaster workshop to do it for you. Using wet plaster or a recommended glue, insert the missing section and leave to dry. Seal it thoroughly and apply gesso or primer as required.

Wood

When restoring a wooden frame or table, fill any cracks and holes with putty or wood filler. Leave to dry and sand down, then apply gesso or primer as required. It is a difficult and costly undertaking to make accurate pieces for any missing sections of a wooden frame. Try using the method described for plaster and insert the piece using a recommended glue.

Metal

Replacing missing pieces on metal objects is best done by a qualified craftsperson. Remove any rust with steel wool or wet-and-dry sandpaper. Remove any heavy deposits with a wire brush and detergent.

Any cracks and holes that do not affect the structure can be filled with car body repair filler. Leave to dry and sand down. Prime with the appropriate metal primer.

Conservation

There are two ways of conserving antiques. The first is to restore them so that they do not look new but retain their naturally aged beauty. If an item is very old and valuable, the task is best left to a conservator. The second form of conservation is to make sure the item is kept in a place and atmosphere that will not affect its appearance or value, such as ensuring your pieces are not positioned in direct sunlight.

THE GILDED ROOM

Gilding, with its varying effects, is still one of the most popular forms of interior decoration and is indeed among the oldest. It improves with age and gives an immediate appearance of opulence.

OPULENT INTERIORS

G ilding has been used in interior decoration for centuries. Gilded interiors immediately evoke the opulence of baroque and rococo salons, and the great palaces of Russia and France. The palace at Versailles was built for the glory of Louis XIV, and its gilded splendor was created as the antithesis of the gloomy palace at the Louvre. In Russia, astounding examples of gilded interiors exist in all their glory, having withstood both

Above: Take a cue from historic pieces when applying gilding. This chair has been lined with gilded decoration.

time and political turmoil. Splendid examples can be seen in Moscow, and in St. Petersburg the Summer Palace remains as one of the truly remarkable examples of gilded interiors.

Today, many modern architects and furniture designers are experimenting with traditional and contemporary gilding effects, and gold detail can be used to great effect in historic and modern interiors alike. In your own home, you can try using traditional methods, or more adventurous touches, with materials such as composition leaf. Basic wooden items such as curtain poles and pelmets can be embellished with gold leaf, and combined with rich drapes of velvet, for a look of theatrical extravagance. Simple modern pieces of furniture can be given the illusion of an antique by the clever application of distressed leaf, aged with acrylic varnish. Old junk shop finds, that

Left: Gilded architectural details frame this doorway in the Palace at Ostankino, Moscow.

Above: The White Room in the House of Friendship, Moscow. The yellow brocade on the walls adds further luster to the gilded details.

Right: In the Peacock Room, designed by James MacNeil Whistler, Art Nouveau-style designs are enhanced by gilded finishes.

might normally be discarded, can be given a new lease on life with such a treatment. Plaster and wooden architectural details can also be given the gold treatment, and can be a very cost effective way of creating a feeling of classic grandeur. Many shops now specialize in plaster reproductions, and special shops can match and renovate original moldings. Whether you wish to create a modern or ancestral look, gilding is a wonderful technique to experiment with.

GILDED CHAIR

An inexpensive Louis XIV-style wooden chair has

first been lacquered and then decorative details have

been applied in real gold leaf. The gilded chair makes

a luxurious centerpiece for your gilded room,

conjuring up images of the splendor of the court of

the Sun King at Versailles. Gild a single chair as a

focal point, or a whole set for real opulence ⌒

YOU WILL NEED

wooden Louis XIV-style
  chair frame
white acrylic primer
1-inch paintbrushes
gray lacquer undercoat
dark green lacquer paint
cotton rags
talc
string
soft brush
water-based size
24-carat loose gold leaf

gilder's pad
gilder's knife
petroleum jelly
gilder's tip
cotton balls
burnishing brush or soft cloth
steel wool
methylated spirit
batting
transparent shellac polish

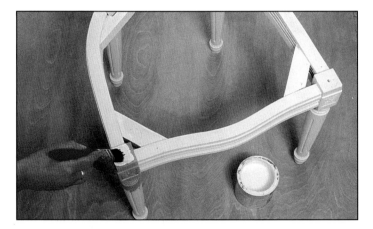

1 Prime the chair frame with acrylic primer and leave to dry for 1 to 2 hours.

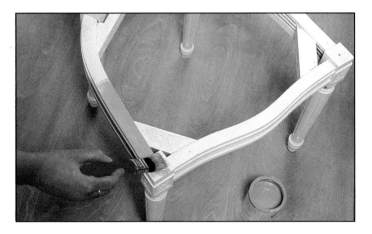

2 Paint on a coat of gray lacquer undercoat and leave to dry for 4 hours.

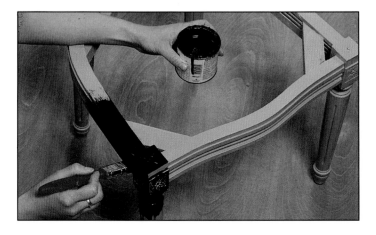

3 Paint on one or two coats of dark green lacquer paint and leave each coat to dry for at least 6 to 8 hours, or overnight if possible.

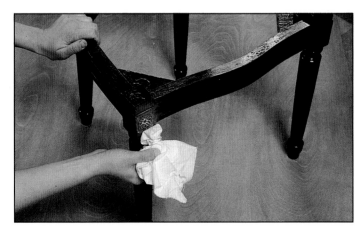

4 Fill a rag with talc and close up with string to make a pounce bag. Pounce the areas to be gilded and brush off the excess talc. ➤

5 Paint a thin, even coat of water-based size onto the areas to be gilded and leave for 20 to 30 minutes, until the size becomes clear and tacky.

6 Blow a sheet of gold leaf onto the gilder's pad, cutting into smaller pieces with a gilder's knife if required. Brush petroleum jelly on the inside of your forearm and lightly brush the gilder's tip over the petroleum jelly. Use the tip to pick up the leaf.

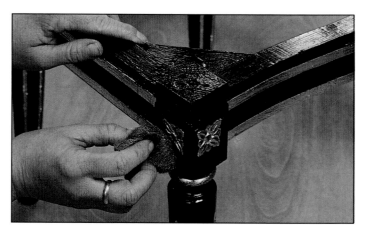

7 Lay the leaf on the sized area of the chair and gently press into place with cotton balls. Continue until the whole sized area is covered with gold leaf.

8 Burnish with a burnishing brush or soft cloth to remove the excess leaf. Dip some steel wool into a little methylated spirit and rub gently on the areas of detail to remove a little of the leaf. Take care not to rub too hard.

9 Make a polishing rubber by covering some batting with a clean rag, leaving an opening at the top. Add a few drops of polish to soak the batting. Close up the rag with string, and when the liquid soaks through, start rubbing the gilded areas. The surface can be buffed with a soft cloth when dry.

RENAISSANCE FRAME

This lovely antique-looking mirror, with its intricately molded frame, has been decorated using the tricky but beautiful water gilding technique. The delicate look of this type of gilding is ideal for pieces of this kind and for restoring old frames to their former glory ⬭

YOU WILL NEED

ready-made gesso in white and red	petroleum jelly
bain marie or double boiler	gilder's tip
wooden picture frame	cotton balls
assorted bristle brushes	agate burnisher
water-based size	steel wool
24-carat loose gold leaf	batting
gilder's pad	cotton rag
	transparent shellac polish
	string

1 Heat the ready-made white gesso in a bain marie or double boiler for 5 minutes. Paint a coat of gesso onto the picture frame and leave to dry for 1 to 2 hours.

2 Heat the ready-made red gesso in the same way and paint up to eight coats of gesso onto the frame, leaving each coat to dry for 1 to 2 hours before applying the next.

3 Paint on a thin, even coat of water-based size and leave for 20 to 30 minutes, until it becomes clear and tacky.

4 Blow a sheet of gold leaf onto the gilder's pad. Brush some petroleum jelly on the inside of your forearm and lightly brush the gilder's tip over the petroleum jelly. Use the tip to pick up the whole sheet.

➤

5 Lay the leaf on the frame and gently press into place with cotton balls. Continue until the whole frame is covered.

6 Burnish with an agate burnisher to remove the excess leaf. Take care not to rub too hard, since this will damage the gesso and spoil the finished effect.

7 To create a distressed effect in keeping with the antique appearance of the frame, gently rub the areas of detail with steel wool to remove a little of the leaf. Take care not to rub too hard.

8 Make a polishing rubber by covering some batting with a clean rag, leaving an opening at the top. Add a few drops of polish to soak the batting. Close up the rag with string, and when the liquid soaks through, start rubbing the gilding. The surface can be buffed with a soft cloth when dry.

BEDSIDE TABLE

This lovely little table has been decorated with real

gold leaf using the versatile oil-gilding technique,

which can be used to gild most surfaces. The delicate

look of the piece has been retained by not gilding the

entire table, but by concentrating on specific areas and

details such as the top and the drawer knob ∞

YOU WILL NEED

small fiberboard bedside table	soft 2-inch paintbrush
cotton rags	burnishing brush or soft cloth
talc	steel wool
string	methylated spirit
soft brush	batting
1-inch paintbrush	transparent shellac polish
water-based size	
24-carat loose gold leaf	
gilder's pad	
gilder's knife	
petroleum jelly	
gilder's tip	

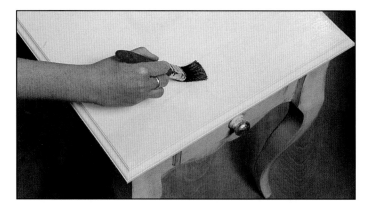

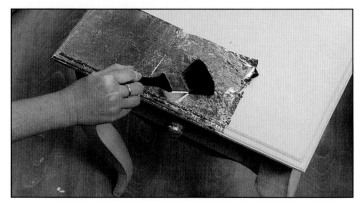

1 Fill a cotton rag with talc and close up with string to make a pounce bag. Pounce the areas to be gilded and brush off the excess talc with a soft brush. Paint a thin, even coat of water-based size onto the areas to be gilded and leave for 20 to 30 minutes, until it becomes clear and tacky. Blow a sheet of gold leaf onto the gilder's pad.

2 Brush some petroleum jelly on the inside of your forearm and lightly brush the gilder's tip over the petroleum jelly. Use the tip to pick up the whole sheet and lay it on the sized areas. Continue working in squares until the whole area is covered. Gently press into place with a soft paintbrush.

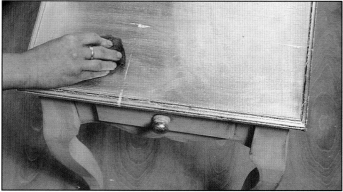

3 Burnish the surface with a burnishing brush or soft cloth to remove the excess leaf until the tabletop is smooth. Dip some steel wool into a little methylated spirit and rub gently over the surface and rim of the table to remove a little of the leaf. Take care not to rub too hard.

4 Make a polishing rubber by covering some batting with a clean rag, leaving an opening at the top. Add small drops of polish to soak the batting. Close up the rag with string, and when the liquid soaks through, start rubbing the gilded areas. The surface can be buffed with a soft cloth when dry.

SHELL FRAME

Shells are ideal objects for gilding, which brings out their natural detail. Using them to adorn frames and mirrors gives the illusion of carvings reminiscent of the baroque interiors. In another context, they can be used to transform a tired old bathroom or kitchen shelf

YOU WILL NEED

assorted sea shells

red oxide spray primer

1/2-inch bristle brushes

water-based size

Dutch metal leaf in gold and
   aluminum

burnishing brush or soft cloth

amber shellac varnish

acrylic varnish

acrylic paints in pale blue,

pink and orange

paint pans

soft cloths

gilded frame

white glue

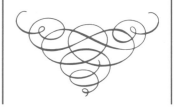

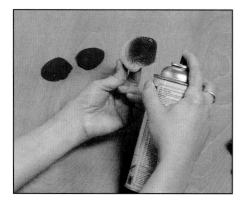

1 Spray the shells with an even coat of red oxide spray primer and leave to dry for 30 minutes to 1 hour.

2 Paint on a thin, even coat of water-based size and leave for 20 to 30 minutes, until it becomes clear and tacky.

3 Gild the shells with gold or aluminum Dutch metal leaf. Burnish with a burnishing brush or soft cloth to remove the excess leaf.

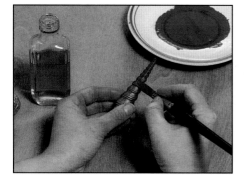

4 Seal the gold shells with a thin, even coat of amber shellac varnish and leave to dry for 45 minutes to 1 hour. Seal the aluminum shells with acrylic varnish and leave to dry for 1 hour.

5 Mix some pale blue acrylic paint with a little water. Paint onto the shells, then rub off most of the paint with a cloth, allowing only a little paint to remain in the areas of detail. Color some of the shells in pink and orange. Leave to dry for 30 minutes.

6 Arrange the shells on the gilded frame and attach with white glue. Leave to dry thoroughly before hanging in place.

WOODEN DRAWER KNOBS

These plain and simple wooden knobs have been decorated with two gilding techniques, both using inexpensive gold composite Dutch metal. The first technique gives the knobs a distressed look, while the second imitates rust

YOU WILL NEED

wooden drawer or doorknobs

red oxide spray primer

1-inch paintbrush

water-based size

broken gold Dutch metal leaf
   (schlag) or gold Dutch metal leaf

burnishing brush or soft cloth

water-based matte varnish

paint pans

powder pigment in burnt umber
   and yellow-ochre

bristle brushes

amber shellac varnish (optional)

1/2-inch varnishing brush
   (optional)

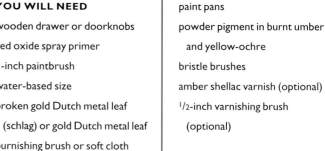

1 Working in a well-ventilated area, spray the knobs with red oxide spray primer. Leave to dry for 1 hour.

2 Paint on a thin, even coat of water-based size and leave for 20 to 30 minutes, until it becomes clear and tacky.

3 One way of gilding the knobs is to sprinkle broken gold Dutch metal leaf onto the surface. Burnish with a burnishing brush or soft cloth to remove the excess leaf and bring up the luster.

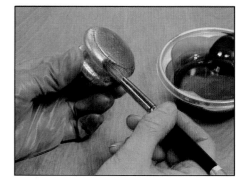

4 Alternatively, gild the knobs with sheets of gold Dutch metal leaf to cover the entire area. Burnish with a burnishing brush or soft cloth to remove any loose leaf and bring up the luster. Pour some water-based varnish into two paint pans.

5 Add burnt umber pigment to one saucer and yellow-ochre pigment to the other. Using a separate brush for each color, dab on patches of the two colors to build up the rust effect, allowing some of the gold to show through. Leave to dry for 1 to 2 hours.

6 The use of varnish with the pigment will seal the surface, so there is no need for further sealing, but you can apply a thin, even coat of amber shellac varnish if you wish. Leave to dry for 1 hour.

PLASTER CORBEL

This baroque-style plaster corbel has been decorated using the water-gilding technique to retain the beauty of the architectural detail. Plaster pieces like this one are available from special suppliers who can help when you need replacements for broken pieces at home

YOU WILL NEED

plaster corbel

white glue

1-inch paintbrush

ready-made red gesso

bain marie or double boiler

methylated spirit

jar

acrylic bristle brush

24-carat loose gold leaf

cotton balls

agate burnisher

steel wool

batting

cotton rag

transparent shellac polish

string

1 Mix two parts white glue with one part water and use to seal the corbel. Leave to dry for 2 hours. Heat the gesso in a bain marie or double boiler. Paint the corbel with up to eight coats of gesso, leaving it to dry for 1 to 2 hours between coats.

2 Make some gilding water by adding a little methylated spirit to some water in a jar until the water is slightly colored. Paint a small area of the corbel with the gilding water.

3 Working with one piece at a time, lay each piece of gold leaf carefully on the damp surface, pressing gently into place with cotton balls. Work the leaf well into the areas of detail.

4 Continue painting small areas with gilding water and applying gold leaf until the whole corbel is covered. Burnish carefully with an agate burnisher. Do not damage the gesso underneath.

5 Distress the surface by gently rubbing with steel wool, taking care not to rub too hard. Concentrate on the areas in relief, to simulate natural wear and tear.

6 Make a polishing rubber by covering some batting with a clean rag. Add a few drops of polish to soak the batting. Close up the rag with string and when the liquid soaks through, rub the gilded surface.

Lamp Base

This simple ceramic lamp base is gilded in three

colors of Dutch metal leaf to give it a contemporary

feel that would lend itself to a modern interior. It is

then enhanced with a verdigris paint finish. Gild

a lampshade to match ∽

YOU WILL NEED

ceramic lamp base

masking tape

sandpaper

white acrylic primer

1-inch paintbrushes

dark green latex paint

water-based size

pencil (optional)

Dutch metal leaf in silver, gold
  and copper

burnishing brush or soft cloth

steel wool

methylated spirit

water-based varnishing wax

viridian-green acrylic paint

soft cloth

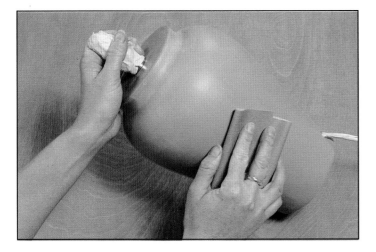

1 Mask off the fittings and lead with masking tape and sand down the surface of the lamp base to provide a tooth for the paint to adhere to.

2 Prime the base with white acrylic primer and leave to dry for 1 to 2 hours. Paint the base with two coats of dark green latex, leaving each coat to dry for 2 to 3 hours.

3 Paint a thin coat of water-based size on to the top section of the base. (Draw a guide line around the top if necessary.) Leave for 20 to 30 minutes, until the size becomes clear and tacky.

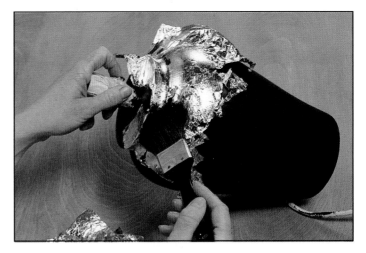

4 Gild the top section of the base with silver Dutch metal leaf. Burnish the surface with a burnishing brush or soft cloth to remove the excess leaf.

➤

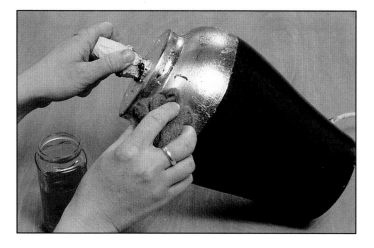

5 Dip some steel wool into a little methylated spirit and gently rub to distress the surface.

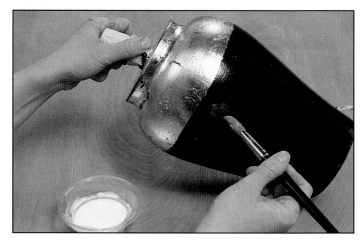

6 Size the bottom half of the base and leave for 20 to 30 minutes until clear and tacky.

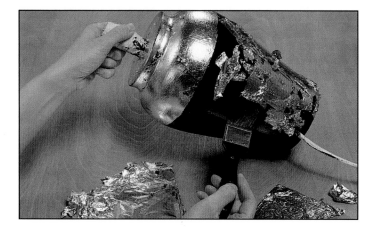

7 Gently crush the gold and copper leaf in your hands and apply randomly over the surface, allowing plenty of base coat to show through. When the surface is covered, burnish with a burnishing brush or soft cloth.

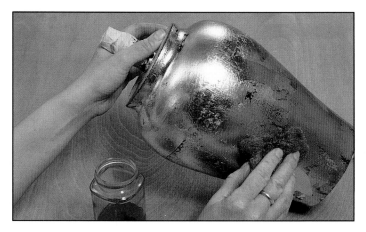

8 Distress the bottom half of the base with steel wool dipped in a little methylated spirit.

9 Seal the entire surface with a thin, even coat of varnishing wax and leave to dry for 1 hour.

10 Mix some viridian-green paint with a little water and paint onto the surface. Rub off most of the paint with a cloth.

PLASTER DECORATIONS

Decorating a plain wall with plaster shapes is

unusual in itself, but adding gilding to the shapes

will make them even more stunning and individual.

The shapes can be applied directly to a wall, or on

small decorative panels or doors ∾

YOU WILL NEED

plaster shapes	plumbline
white glue	acrylic paints in yellow-ochre
assorted decorator's brushes	and rose
waterproof ceramic adhesive	acrylic scumble glaze
masking tape	paint pans
white acrylic wood primer	water-based size
white latex paint	gold Dutch metal leaf
ruler	burnishing brush or soft cloth
	water-based varnishing wax

1 Mix two parts white glue with one part water and seal the plaster shapes with this mixture, working the sealant into the recesses. Leave to dry for 2 hours.

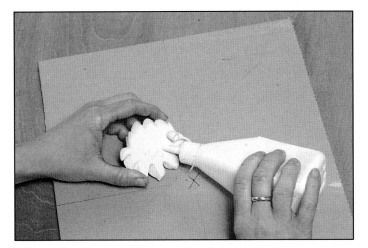

2 Use a thick, even coat of ceramic adhesive to stick the shapes to the panel or wall. Leave to dry for 3 to 4 hours. Hold the shapes in place with masking tape while the glue is drying, if necessary.

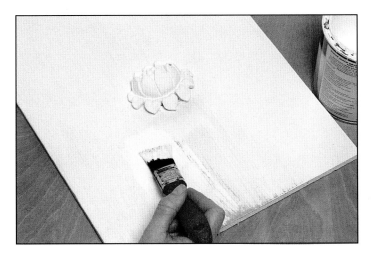

3 Paint the panel or wall and shapes with a coat of white acrylic primer and leave to dry for 1 to 2 hours. Paint on a coat of white latex and leave to dry for 2 to 3 hours.

4 Measure out the positions of the stripes on the panel or wall. Use a ruler or plumbline to mask off the first stripe with masking tape. Reduce the tackiness of the masking tape on a piece of cloth first. ➤

5 Mix one part yellow-ochre acrylic paint with six parts scumble glaze. Apply to the area between the masking tape using random brush strokes and allowing plenty of the base color to show through the glaze. Leave to dry for 2 to 3 hours.

6 Remove the masking tape and remask along the outside edge of the glazed stripe. Mix one part rose acrylic paint with six parts scumble glaze. Paint the second stripe in the same way as the first and leave to dry for 2 to 3 hours.

7 Paint a thin, even coat of water-based size onto the plaster shapes, working it into the recesses, and leave for 20 to 30 minutes, until it becomes clear and tacky.

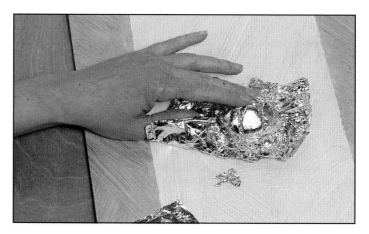

8 Place a sheet of gold Dutch metal leaf onto the sized surface and press lightly into the detail, smoothing with your fingers and ensuring that the whole shape is covered.

9 Burnish the shapes with a burnishing brush or soft cloth to remove the excess leaf.

10 Seal with a thin, even coat of water-based varnishing wax and leave to dry.

CORNER CUPBOARD

This gothic-style wooden corner cupboard has been gilded using aluminum Dutch metal leaf on a blue base coat. The cupboard retains its historical feel and the gilding process creates the illusion of steel, creating a timeless yet contemporary piece

YOU WILL NEED

wooden corner cupboard

royal-blue latex paint

1-inch paintbrushes

water-based size

aluminum Dutch metal leaf

burnishing brush or soft cloth

steel wool

methylated spirit

water-based flat varnish

viridian-green acrylic paint

paint pan

soft cloth

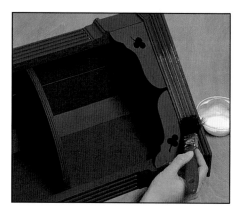

1 Paint the cupboard with royal-blue latex, making sure the whole surface and any details are well covered, and leave to dry for 2 to 3 hours. Apply a second coat and leave to dry.

2 Paint on a thin, even coat of water-based size and leave for 20 to 30 minutes, until it becomes clear and tacky.

3 Gild the cupboard with aluminum Dutch metal leaf, making sure the whole surface is covered. Burnish with a burnishing brush or soft cloth to remove the excess leaf.

4 Dip some steel wool into a little methylated spirit and lightly rub the edges and areas of detail to reveal some of the base coat beneath the aluminum leaf. Seal with water-based flat varnish and leave to dry for about 3 hours.

5 Mix some viridian-green acrylic paint with a little water and paint onto the surface. Working quickly, rub off most of the paint with a soft cloth, leaving only a little paint in the areas of detail. Use a clean area of cloth each time or you will rub the color back on.

STENCILED HEART CUSHION

A simple cushion can be transformed by stenciling

with fabric paints to make a unique accessory.

A collection of cushions, all slightly different but

made on the same theme, will brighten up your

sitting room or bedroom

YOU WILL NEED

fabric squares, 18 x 18 inches	cutting mat
masking tape	drawing pins
gold fabric paint	iron
small paintbrush	needle and matching thread
pencil	12-inch zipper
paper	cushion pad, 12 x 12 inches
stencil cardboard	2 yards fringe
scalpel or craft knife	

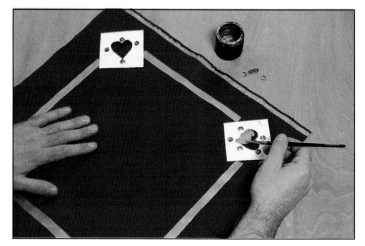

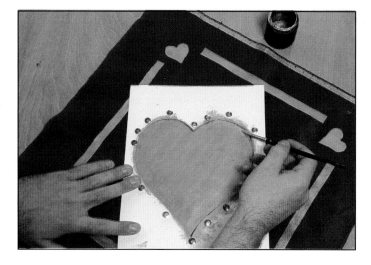

1 Mask off a border on one fabric square with masking tape. Each edge should be approximately 9 inches long and ½ inch wide, with a gap at each corner for the heart motif. Apply two coats of fabric paint between the masked areas, leaving the first coat to dry thoroughly before applying the next.

2 Trace the small heart template from the back of the book and transfer to four pieces of stencil cardboard. Cut out the four hearts with a scalpel or craft knife on a cutting mat. Using drawing pins, pin them in place in the gaps in the border so that they point toward the center. Apply two coats of fabric paint through each stencil, leaving the first coat to dry thoroughly before applying the next.

3 Trace the large heart template from the back of the book and cut from stencil cardboard. Pin firmly in the center of the fabric. Apply three coats of gold fabric paint, allowing each coat to dry thoroughly before applying the next. Using a hot iron, press the reverse of the fabric to fix the paint. Sew together the cushion, insert the zipper and cushion pad and decorate with fringe.

APPLIQUÉ STAR CUSHION

This sumptuous cushion is quite simple to make.
It uses an appliqué technique, with the pieces first
painted with gold fabric paint. The bold design would
complement any interior and makes a beautifully
individual gift. The simple yet effective shapes could
be repeated on a throw or the border of a curtain, or
even stenciled in gold on a wall ∞

YOU WILL NEED

pencil
scalpel or craft knife
cutting mat
card
1 yard white canvas
gold fabric paint
small paintbrush
iron
scissors
fabric glue
2 blue fabric squares,
   10 x 10 inches

2 burgundy fabric squares,
   10 x 10 inches
button blank
sewing machine
matching threads
fabric square, 18 x 18 inches,
   for the back
12-inch zipper
cushion pad, 12 x 12 inches
2 yards fringe

1 Trace the star template from the back of the book. Using a scalpel or craft knife on a cutting mat, cut out a star from cardboard. Draw around the cardboard template four times on canvas.

2 Paint the stars and a small gold circle for covering the button with two coats of gold fabric paint. Using a hot iron, press the reverse of the canvas to fix the paint, then cut out the stars and circle.

3 Using fabric glue, stick a star into the center of each of the four fabric squares and leave to dry. Cover the button blank with the gold circle.

4 Sew around the stars using a zigzag stitch. Join the squares together to make one large square. Sew together the cushion, and insert the zipper and pad. Sew on the fringe and the button.

CURTAIN POLE AND PELMET

Simple fiberboard pelmets and plain wooden curtain poles are radically transformed by gilding. As they are quite large, using Dutch metal leaf will considerably reduce the cost of the project. Try experimenting with combinations of the available colors to create different effects

YOU WILL NEED

plain wooden curtain pole
 and rings

red oxide spray primer

water-based size

assorted decorator's brushes

Dutch metal leaf in copper,
 aluminum and gold

burnishing brush or soft cloth

acrylic varnishing wax

plain fiberboard pelmet

red oxide paint

steel wool

methylated spirit

amber shellac varnish

red acrylic paint

paint pan

soft cloth

CURTAIN POLE

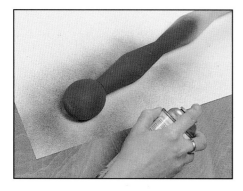

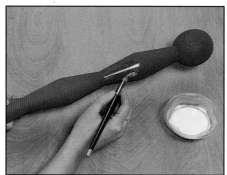

1 Spray an even coat of red oxide primer over the curtain pole and rings and leave to dry for 1 hour.

2 Paint a thin, even coat of water-based size on to the sections of the pole to be gilded in copper. Leave for 20 to 30 minutes, until the size becomes clear and tacky.

3 Gild the sized areas with copper Dutch metal leaf. Burnish with a burnishing brush or cloth to remove the excess leaf.

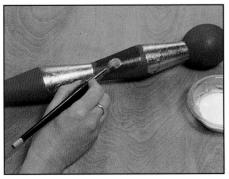

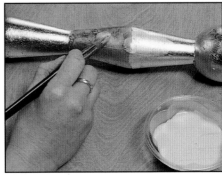

4 Size the remaining sections of the pole and leave for 20 to 30 minutes, until the size becomes clear and tacky.

5 Gild with aluminum Dutch metal leaf and burnish with a burnishing brush or cloth to remove the excess leaf.

6 Seal the curtain pole with two coats of acrylic varnishing wax. Leave to dry for 2 to 3 hours between each coat. ➢

PELMET

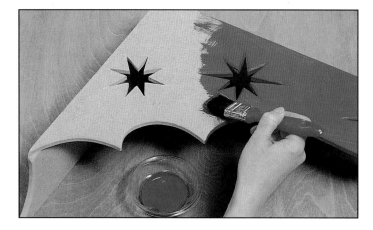

1 Prime the pelmet with a coat of red oxide paint and leave to dry for 2 to 3 hours.

2 Paint a thin, even coat of water-based size on to the pelmet and leave for 20 to 30 minutes, until it becomes clear and tacky.

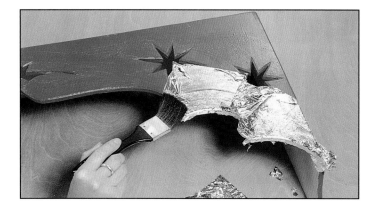

3 Gild the surface of the pelmet with gold Dutch metal leaf. Burnish with a burnishing brush or soft cloth to remove the excess leaf.

4 Dip some steel wool into a little methylated spirit and gently rub the edges where the pelmet would receive natural wear.

5 Seal with a thin, even coat of amber shellac varnish and leave to dry for 45 minutes to 1 hour.

6 Mix some red acrylic paint with a little water. Paint onto the surface and leave to set for 5 minutes. Rub off most of the paint with a cloth, allowing only a little to remain in the areas of detail. Dampen the cloth if the paint has set too much. Leave to dry.

TASSELS AND TIE-BACKS

Here is another unusual way of decorating your windows with gilding. Rope and jute tie-backs are widely available and using gold Dutch metal leaf and metallic sprays to gild them is an inexpensive way to add glamour to your curtains and upholstery

YOU WILL NEED

jute tie-back

2-inch paintbrush

water-based size

large bucket

white glue

red oxide spray primer

1-inch paintbrushes

gold Dutch metal leaf

burnishing brush or soft cloth

amber shellac varnish

jute tassel

copper spray paint

1 Paint the tie-back liberally with water-based size and a 2-inch brush and leave to drain off in a large bucket overnight. Repeat the process and leave to drain and dry again overnight.

2 Dilute two parts white glue with one part water in a large bucket and stir well. Paint the tie-back liberally with the mixture, dunking it into the bucket if necessary to make sure it is completely soaked. Discard the glue mixture and leave the tie-back to drain over the now-empty bucket in a warm place overnight. When dry, the tie-back should be quite hard and crisp.

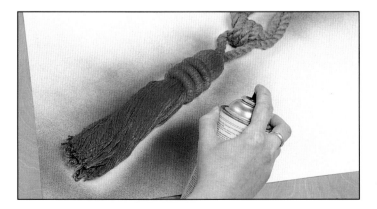

3 Prime the tie-back with red oxide spray primer, making sure that the whole area and any recesses are covered. Leave to dry for 30 minutes to 1 hour.

4 Using a 1-inch brush, paint water-based size over the tie-back, trying to get into all the cracks but avoiding too many bubbles. Leave for 20 to 30 minutes, until the size becomes tacky. ➤

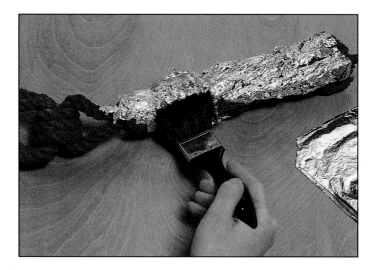

5 Gild the tie-back with gold Dutch metal leaf, getting into as much of the detail as possible. Burnish with a burnishing brush or soft cloth to remove the excess leaf.

6 Seal the tie-back with a thin, even coat of amber shellac varnish and leave to dry for 30 minutes to 1 hour.

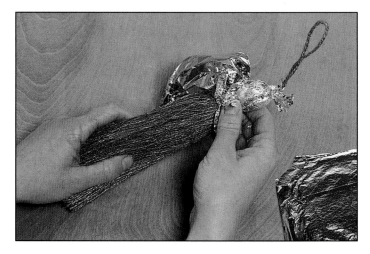

7 Spray the tassel with copper paint, making sure that all the tufts at the base are covered. Leave to dry for 30 minutes and repeat.

8 Paint the top of the tassel with water-based size and leave for 20 to 30 minutes, until it becomes tacky and clear. Gild the top of the tassel and remove the excess leaf with your fingers.

9 Paint the top of the tassel with a thin, even coat of amber shellac varnish and leave to dry for 30 minutes to 1 hour.

BATHROOM ACCESSORIES

This very decadent use of gilding will add an atmosphere of richness and glamour to your bathroom. Using gold Dutch metal leaf is an inexpensive way of transforming cheap basic accessories to make your smallest room into a glittering haven ∽

YOU WILL NEED

plain wooden toilet seat

plain wooden towel rail

plain wooden toilet tissue holder

sandpaper

white acrylic wood primer

1-inch paintbrushes

red oxide spray primer

water-based size

gold Dutch metal leaf

burnishing brush or soft cloth

steel wool

methylated spirit

water-based acrylic varnish

gold tassels

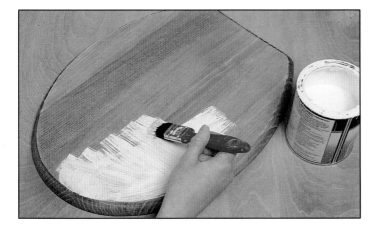

1 Sand off any coating on the wood of the toilet seat and accessories to provide a tooth for the paint. Prime the surfaces with acrylic wood primer and leave to dry for 1 to 2 hours.

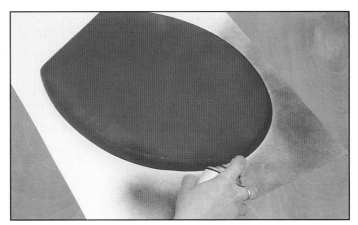

2 Spray an even coat of red oxide primer over the toilet seat and accessories, making sure all the surfaces are evenly coated. Leave to dry for 1 hour.

3 Paint a thin coat of water-based size on the entire surface of the toilet seat and leave for 20 to 30 minutes, until the size becomes clear and tacky.

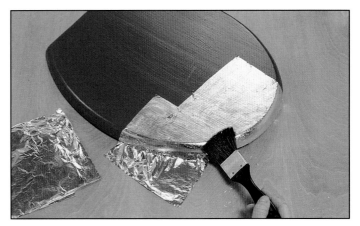

4 Gild the entire surface of the toilet seat with gold Dutch metal leaf. Burnish with a burnishing brush or soft cloth to remove the excess leaf. ➤

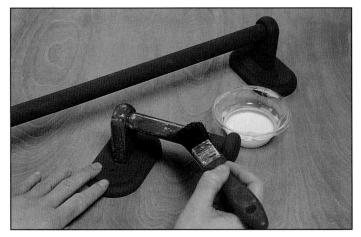

5 Dip some steel wool into a little methylated spirit and gently rub the edges where the wood would receive natural wear. Seal the whole surface with water-based acrylic varnish and leave to dry .

6 Size the towel rail and toilet tissue holder and leave for 20 to 30 minutes, until the size becomes clear and tacky.

7 Gild the accessories with gold Dutch metal leaf and burnish.

8 Distress the accessories with steel wool and methylated spirit.

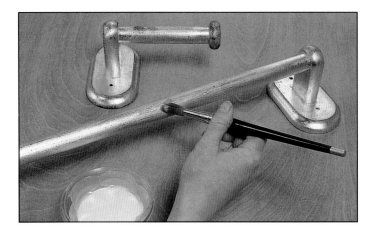

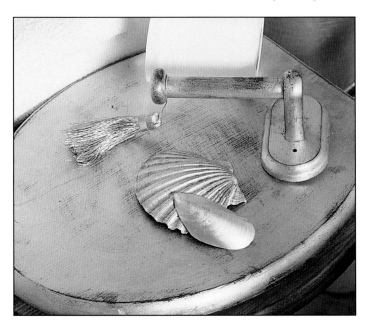

9 Seal with water-based acrylic varnish. Hang gold tassels from the ends of the accessories to add extra glamour.

Right: Gilded accessories.

Heraldic Tiles

Tiles are a joy to gild, since the ceramic surface is so smooth. This is a quick and easy way of creating a luxurious decor in your bathroom or kitchen or of rejuvenating existing tiles. Sealing the tiles after gilding makes them hard-wearing and waterproof, so that they will look wonderful for years

YOU WILL NEED

ceramic tiles
stencil cardboard
pencil
scalpel or craft knife
cutting mat
masking tape
soft cloths
water-based size
1-inch paintbrushes
Dutch metal leaf in aluminum,
copper and gold
burnishing brush or soft cloth
stencil brush
water-based varnishing wax or
flat varnish

1 Trace the crown and fleur-de-lys templates from the back of the book and transfer on to the stencil cardboard. Use a scalpel or craft knife to cut out the stencils on a cutting mat.

2 Reduce the tackiness of the masking tape on a piece of cloth, then mask off the border on the tiles.

3 You can prime the tiles if desired, but a pleasing effect is created by allowing the color of the tiles to show through. To gild a whole tile, paint a thin, even coat of water-based size over the entire surface and leave for 20 to 30 minutes, until it becomes tacky.

4 Crush some aluminum Dutch metal leaf gently in your hand and apply randomly to the surface, so that some of the tile shows through. Burnish with a burnishing brush or soft cloth to remove the excess leaf, taking care not to rub too hard. ➤

5 To gild the borders, paint a coat of size around the edge of the tile, up to the masking tape. Leave the size for 20 to 30 minutes until it becomes tacky and clear.

6 Place a stencil in the center of the tile. Using a stencil brush, stipple water-based size through the stencil. Leave for 20 to 30 minutes until it becomes tacky and clear.

7 Gild the fleur-de-lys design and borders with copper Dutch metal leaf. Burnish with a burnishing brush or soft cloth to remove the excess leaf, taking care not to rub too hard.

8 Gild the crown design and borders with gold Dutch metal leaf. Burnish with a burnishing brush or soft cloth to remove the excess leaf, taking care not to rub too hard.

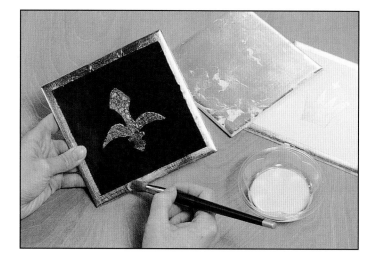

9 Seal the tiles with water-based varnishing wax or flat varnish. If using wax, leave to dry for 1 hour, then buff with a cloth. If using varnish, you may need to apply two coats, allowing 2 hours drying time between each coat.

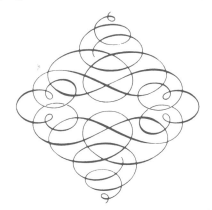

GOLD, GOLD, EVERYWHERE

Gilding does not have to be confined to traditional objects. It can be used on many different surfaces, and will give the most unassuming and inexpensive item a new lease on life.

DECORATIVE ITEMS

*J*ust one gilded item in a room can create a simple yet impressive touch of glamour. Almost anything can be gilded, so scour junk shops and flea markets for supposed lost causes, and see how fantastic the results can be. Mass-produced items can also be given an individual touch – a simple candlestick can be bought cheaply, and may be the perfect candidate for the gold treatment. Since candlesticks, both traditional and modern, are available in interesting shapes, they provide a wonderful surface to work on. Small items also allow you the liberty of trying out different effects – whether you are aiming for a classic result, or a contemporary look. Transform a simple wooden or cardboard box with gold leaf, powders or pastes, to create a glorious gift box or storage box for precious secrets.

With new materials arriving on the market, you can create the look without using the more lengthy traditional methods, making gilding easier and quicker to achieve than ever before. The key is to be imaginative – and brave – when considering what to gild. No matter how unlikely the object first seems, keep your eyes open to the potential of the technique, and go for gold.

Above: A carved wooden frame was first gilded with Dutch metal leaf, and then embellished with tassels and plaster decorations.

Right: Gold powder was used to decorate this sun-burst mirror.

Below: Aluminum leaf adds luster to a wooden candlestick.

Above: Strong, contemporary shapes are the perfect foil for gilding.

PLANT URN

It is hard to believe that this beautiful piece came from humble beginnings, but it started life as a simple plastic plant urn. The use of Dutch metal leaf makes the urn inexpensive to gild, and the technique makes it easy to produce an item of beauty that you won't want to keep outdoors

YOU WILL NEED

plastic plant urn

sandpaper

red oxide spray primer

water-based size

assorted bristle brushes

gold Dutch metal leaf

burnishing brush or soft cloth

steel wool

methylated spirit

amber shellac varnish

acrylic paints in pale blue and gray

paint pan

soft cloth

1 Sand the surface of the urn to provide a tooth for the paint to adhere to. Spray with red oxide spray primer and leave to dry.

2 Paint on a thin, even coat of water-based size and leave for 20 to 30 minutes, until it becomes clear and tacky.

3 Carefully lay the gold Dutch metal leaf on to the surface to cover the whole area. Burnish with a burnishing brush or soft cloth to remove the excess leaf and bring up the luster.

4 Dip some steel wool into a little methylated spirit and gently rub the raised areas and details of the urn to distress the surface, taking care not to rub too hard.

5 Seal with a thin, even coat of amber shellac varnish and leave to dry for 45 minutes to 1 hour.

6 Mix the blue and gray acrylic paint with a little water. Paint the surface and leave to set for 5 minutes. Rub off most of the paint with a cloth, allowing only a little paint to remain in the areas of detail. Dampen the cloth if the paint has set too much. Leave to dry.

LAMPSHADE

A simple parchment lampshade makes an ideal base for gilding. This stenciled design on a shellac base coat gives the shade an antique appearance. Remember to use a low-wattage bulb with this shade to avoid tarnishing

YOU WILL NEED

plain parchment lampshade

stencil brushes

amber shellac varnish

pencil

stencil cardboard

scalpel or craft knife

cutting mat

masking tape

gold stencil paint

1 Using a large round stencil brush, stipple an even but blotchy coat of amber shellac varnish over the surface of the lampshade and leave to dry for 30 minutes to 1 hour.

2 Trace the templates from the back of the book and transfer onto stencil cardboard.

3 Cut out the stencils with a scalpel or craft knife on a cutting mat. It is easier if you move the stencil toward the blade when cutting.

4 Mark the positions for the stencils around the lampshade. Secure the first stencil at the bottom of the shade with masking tape. Stir the gold paint well, then stipple through the stencil. Do not load the brush with too much paint or it will bleed. Remove the stencil carefully before repositioning the next one.

5 When you have completed the bottom row, secure the second stencil at the top of the shade with masking tape. Stencil the top row in the same way as before and leave the shade to dry for at least 1 hour before using.

HEAD OF MARS

Plaster copies of details from famous statues are now widely available and are relatively inexpensive, as well as easy to gild. This head of Mars has been gilded using copper Dutch metal leaf. The gilding was then enhanced with a verdigris finish to give an antique appearance

YOU WILL NEED

plaster head
white glue
1-inch paintbrushes
deep red acrylic gesso
water-based size
copper Dutch metal leaf
burnishing brush or soft cloth
steel wool
methylated spirit
water-based varnishing wax

acrylic paints in deep green,
   viridian-green, yellow-ochre
   and white
paint palette
bristle brushes
old sheet or towel
flower mister
whiting (French chalk)
flat acrylic transparent varnish

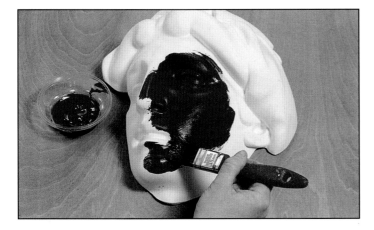

1 Seal the head with a mixture of white glue diluted with one part water. Leave to dry for 2 to 3 hours. Prime the head with a coat of deep red acrylic gesso and leave to dry for 2 hours.

2 Paint on a thin coat of water-based size and leave for 20 to 30 minutes, until it becomes clear and tacky.

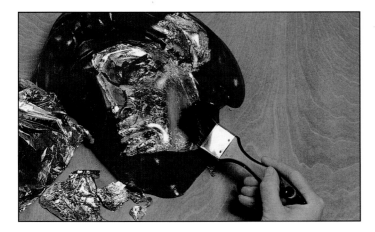

3 Lay copper leaf on to the sized head until the whole surface is covered. Burnish with a burnishing brush or soft cloth to remove the excess leaf and smooth the surface.

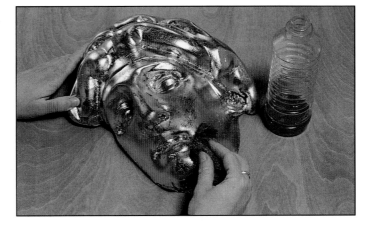

4 Dip some steel wool into a little methylated spirit and gently rub the surface to reveal some of the base coat.

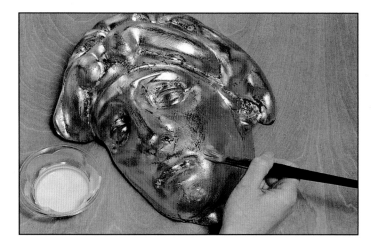

5 Paint a thin, even coat of water-based varnishing wax onto the surface and leave to dry for 1 to 2 hours.

6 To make a verdigris color, mix some deep green and viridian-green acrylic paint with water on a palette. Separately mix some yellow-ochre and white acrylic paint with a little water.

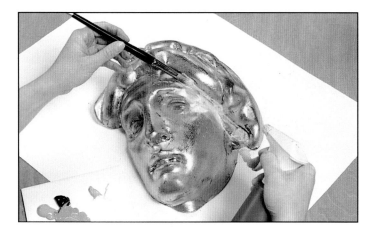

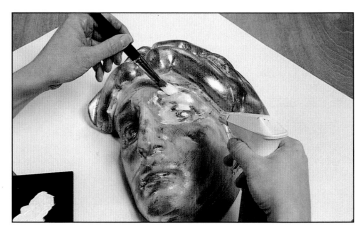

7 Place the head on a sheet or towel. Dab the verdigris mix onto the surface. Working quickly, spray water from the flower mister over the paint to disperse it and so that it dribbles down the head. Dab some off-white color into the details and disperse with water as before.

8 Before the paint dries, dab some whiting (French chalk) into the areas of detail where it will adhere to the damp paint. Brush away any excess whiting and leave the head to dry for 2 hours.

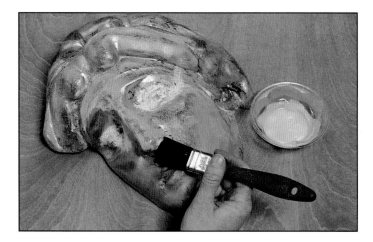

9 Paint the entire surface with acrylic varnish, taking care to cover any recesses and details and leave to dry for 1 to 2 hours.

GILDED VASE

Glass is a lovely surface for gilding, and frosted glass is especially suitable as its slightly rough surface provides the perfect tooth for size. If you are planning to decorate glasses used for drinking, it is not advisable to gild them ⌒

YOU WILL NEED

frosted glass vase

1-inch paintbrush

water-based size

Dutch metal leaf in copper and
   silver

burnishing brush or soft cloth

pencil

stencil cardboard

scalpel or craft knife

cutting mat

stencil brush

water-based varnishing wax

soft cloth

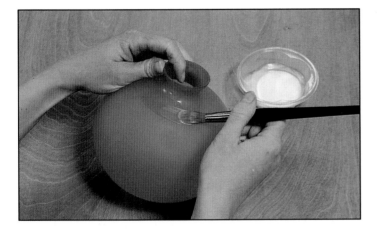

1 Paint a thin coat of water-based size onto the rim and near the bottom edge of the vase. Leave for 20 to 30 minutes, until it becomes clear and tacky. Usually a coat of primer is applied before the size but for this vase it has been omitted to achieve a more delicate look. The vase will wear just as well once sealed.

2 Gild the sized areas with copper Dutch metal leaf. Burnish with a burnishing brush or soft cloth to remove the excess leaf, but be careful not to rub too hard.

3 Trace the template from the back of the book and transfer to stencil cardboard. Cut out with a scalpel or craft knife on a cutting mat.

4 Place the stencil on the vase and stipple through water-based size with a stencil brush. Carefully remove the stencil and leave the size for 20 to 30 minutes, until it becomes clear and tacky. ➤

5 Gild the stenciled crosses with silver Dutch metal leaf and burnish with a burnishing brush or soft cloth.

6 Seal the gilded areas with water-based varnishing wax and leave to dry for about 1 hour. Polish with a soft cloth to bring up the luster.

CANDLESTICK

Candlesticks are available in many different shapes and sizes. They can be given a rich, aged effect with the use of the various shades of Dutch metal leaf. Don't forget to look for candlesticks in junk shops, where you may find more unusual pieces

YOU WILL NEED

wooden candlestick

red oxide spray primer

water-based size

assorted bristle brushes

gold Dutch metal leaf

burnishing brush or soft cloth

steel wool

methylated spirit

amber shellac varnish

acrylic paints in red and
   yellow-ochre

paint pan

soft cloth

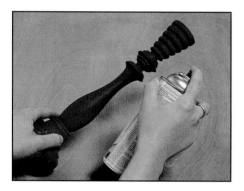

1 Spray the candlestick with an even coat of red oxide spray primer, making sure all the details and recesses are covered. Leave to dry for 30 minutes to 1 hour.

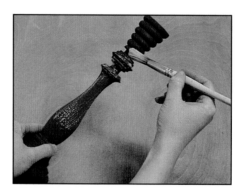

2 Paint on a thin, even coat of water-based size and leave for 20 to 30 minutes, until it becomes clear and tacky.

3 Carefully lay the gold Dutch metal leaf on to the surface to cover the whole area. Burnish with a burnishing brush or soft cloth to remove the excess leaf and bring up the luster.

4 Dip some steel wool into a little methylated spirit and gently rub the raised areas and details of the candlestick to distress the surface, taking care not to rub too hard.

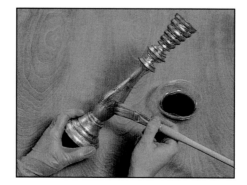

5 Seal with a thin, even coat of amber shellac varnish and leave to dry for 45 minutes to 1 hour.

6 Mix the red and yellow-ochre acrylic paint with a little water. Paint onto the surface and leave to set for 5 minutes. Rub off most of the paint with a cloth, allowing only a little paint to remain in the areas of detail. Dampen the cloth if the paint has set too much. Leave to dry.

PLANT POTS

Ordinary terra-cotta plant pots are pleasing objects in themselves and can be decorated in many ways. Gilded plant pots make attractive bases for fresh or dried flower arrangements. They can also be used for holding candles, which can be secured with florist's foam

YOU WILL NEED

assorted terra-cotta plant pots
red oxide spray primer
water-based size
1-inch bristle brushes
gold Dutch metal leaf
burnishing brush or soft cloth
steel wool
methylated spirit
amber shellac varnish
blue acrylic paint
paint pan
soft cloth

1 Remove any earth or grit and wash the pots well. Leave to dry. Spray with red oxide primer and leave to dry for 30 minutes to 1 hour.

2 Paint on a thin, even coat of water-based size and leave for 20 to 30 minutes, until it becomes clear and tacky.

3 Carefully lay pieces of Dutch metal leaf on to the surfaces to cover the entire area. Burnish with a burnishing brush or soft cloth to remove the excess leaf and bring up the luster.

4 Dip some steel wool into a little methylated spirit and gently rub the gilded plant pots along the rims and the areas where they would suffer natural wear and tear. Take care not to rub too hard.

5 Seal with an even coat of amber shellac varnish and leave to dry for 45 minutes to 1 hour. Mix some blue acrylic paint with a little water. Paint onto the surface and allow to set for 5 minutes. Rub off most of the paint with a cloth, so that only a little paint remains in areas of detail. Dampen the cloth if the paint has set too much.

AMPHORA

This amphora, bought from a garden center, has been

decorated using gilding and a lapis lazuli paint effect

to give it an ancient feel. The dotting of amber shellac

over the amphora creates the illusion of rust on the

surface. The deep ultramarine is reminiscent of the

color favored by the ancient Egyptians ∽

YOU WILL NEED

terra-cotta amphora

pale blue spray paint

acrylic paints in ultramarine,
    black, white, yellow-ochre and
    viridian-green

texture gel

paint pans

large, round stencil brush

pencil (optional)

water-based size

1-inch paintbrushes

gold Dutch metal leaf

burnishing brush or soft cloth

water-based varnishing wax

soft cloths

fine paintbrush

amber French enamel varnish

old stiff-bristled brush

flower mister

old sheet or towel

water-based matte acrylic varnish

1 Wash the amphora, if necessary, and leave to dry. Spray with an even coat of pale blue spray paint, making sure that the whole area is covered. Leave to dry for 1 hour.

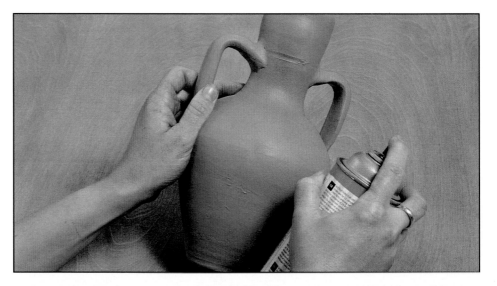

2 Mix some ultramarine acrylic paint with some texture gel. Using a large, round stencil brush, stipple a heavy coat around the bottom half of the amphora. Draw a line around the middle of the amphora if necessary. Leave to dry for 3 hours. The paint should have a hard texture when dry.

3 Paint a thin coat of water-based size onto the top half of the amphora, making sure that the whole area is covered. Leave for 20 to 30 minutes, until it becomes clear and tacky.

4 Gild the sized areas using gold Dutch metal leaf. Burnish with a burnishing brush or soft cloth to remove the excess leaf and continue gilding until the whole area is covered.

5 Paint a thin, even coat of water-based varnishing wax onto the gilded surface. Leave to dry for 2 to 3 hours, then buff with a soft cloth.

6 Using a fine brush, dab some spots of amber French enamel varnish onto the gilded surface to create the illusion of rust. Leave to dry for 30 minutes.

7 Mix some black acrylic paint with a little water. Paint random areas of the bottom part of the pot black, keeping the strokes diagonal. Leave to dry for 1 hour. ➤

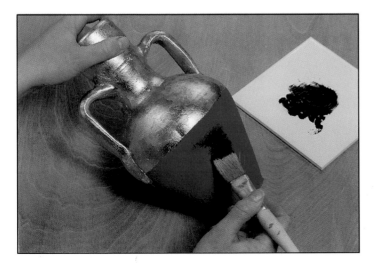

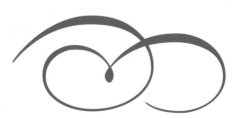

8 Mix some ultramarine acrylic paint with a little white and some water. Paint some more random areas of the bottom part of the pot in this color. Leave to dry for 1 hour.

9 Mix three acrylic colors with water in separate paint pans: yellow-ochre, white and black. Load an old stiff-bristled brush with one color at a time and flick the bristles back to give a fine spray of dots over the surface of the pot.

10 Make a verdigris color by mixing two parts viridian-green acrylic paint with one part white and a little water.

11 Fill the flower mister with water and test the spray. Place the amphora on an old sheet or towel. Paint some verdigris color onto the top half of the amphora and disperse with the flower mister so that the color dribbles down the pot. Continue until you have the desired verdigris effect. Leave to dry for 2 to 3 hours.

12 Paint the whole pot with a thin, even coat of water-based matte varnish. Leave to dry for 2 to 3 hours.

HAT BOX

Plain cardboard gift boxes can be bought in all shapes and sizes from most craft shops and department stores. Sumptuous velvet and gilded cherubs transform the simple box into a beautiful gift for a loved one that will be treasured for years. The box can be used to store many items – not just hats

YOU WILL NEED

plain cardboard gift box

ruler or measuring tape

paper, for pattern

pencil

red velvet

tailor's chalk

scissors

gold taffeta or lining material

white or fabric glue

1/4-inch paintbrush

pins

gold-colored sewing thread

needle

florist's wire

dried flowers and pods

cherub decoration

gold spray paint

bradawl

wire cutters

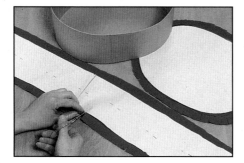

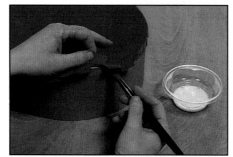

1 Measure the box lid and sides and make paper templates the same size. Transfer onto the velvet using tailor's chalk. Cut around the template, leaving a 1-inch seam allowance all the way around. Cut small slits to the chalk line.

2 Lay the box and lid on the taffeta or lining material and draw two ovals approximately 10 inches larger all around. Glue the first velvet piece to the base of the box, sticking the cut slits to the sides of the box.

3 Next, stick the velvet side piece to the box, painting on the glue and folding over the cut slits to make a neat edge. At the top edge, fold and stick the velvet onto the inside of the box. Repeat with the lid.

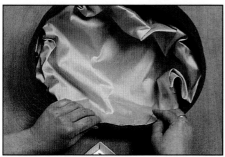

4 Gather the lining piece into the base of the box and pin in place. Using small stitches and gold-colored thread, oversew the lining around the inside edges to hide the rough velvet edges. Repeat with the lining for the lid.

5 Wire the dried flowers and pods together with the cherub in a pleasing arrangement. Spray with gold paint, making sure that the whole area is covered, and leave to dry for 30 minutes.

6 Make two holes in the box with a bradawl. Thread some florist's wire through to the inside of the box, loop over the arrangement and thread through the second hole. Wind the ends of the wire together neatly and trim with wire cutters.

CONTEMPORARY TRAY

This plain wooden tray has been totally transformed into a stylish accessory for a modern home. The contemporary appearance is created by the use of aluminum leaf and bronze powders and is bound to attract admiring comments. When varnished, the tray will stand up to normal wear and tear

YOU WILL NEED

plain wooden tray

dark blue spray paint

water-based size

1-inch paintbrush

aluminum leaf

burnishing brush or soft cloth

pencil

stencil cardboard

scalpel or craft knife

cutting mat

stencil brush

face mask

copper powder

saucer

2-inch paintbrush

acrylic satin varnish

1 Spray the tray with two coats of dark blue spray paint, leaving to dry for 1 hour between coats.

2 Paint a thin, even coat of water-based size onto the top rim of the tray and leave for 20 to 30 minutes, until the size becomes clear and tacky. Gild with aluminum leaf and burnish with a burnishing brush or soft cloth to remove the excess leaf.

3 Trace the templates from the back of the book and transfer to the stencil cardboard. Using a scalpel or craft knife and cutting mat, cut out the stencils.

4 Position the stencils on the base of the tray. Using a stencil brush, stipple water-based size through the stencils. Remove the stencils. Leave for 20 to 30 minutes, until the size becomes clear and tacky.

5 Wearing a mask, tip some copper powder onto a saucer. Pick up some powder with a 2-inch brush and brush over the sized areas. Remove the excess powder with a burnishing brush or soft cloth.

6 Seal the tray with two to three coats of acrylic satin varnish, leaving 2 to 3 hours between coats.

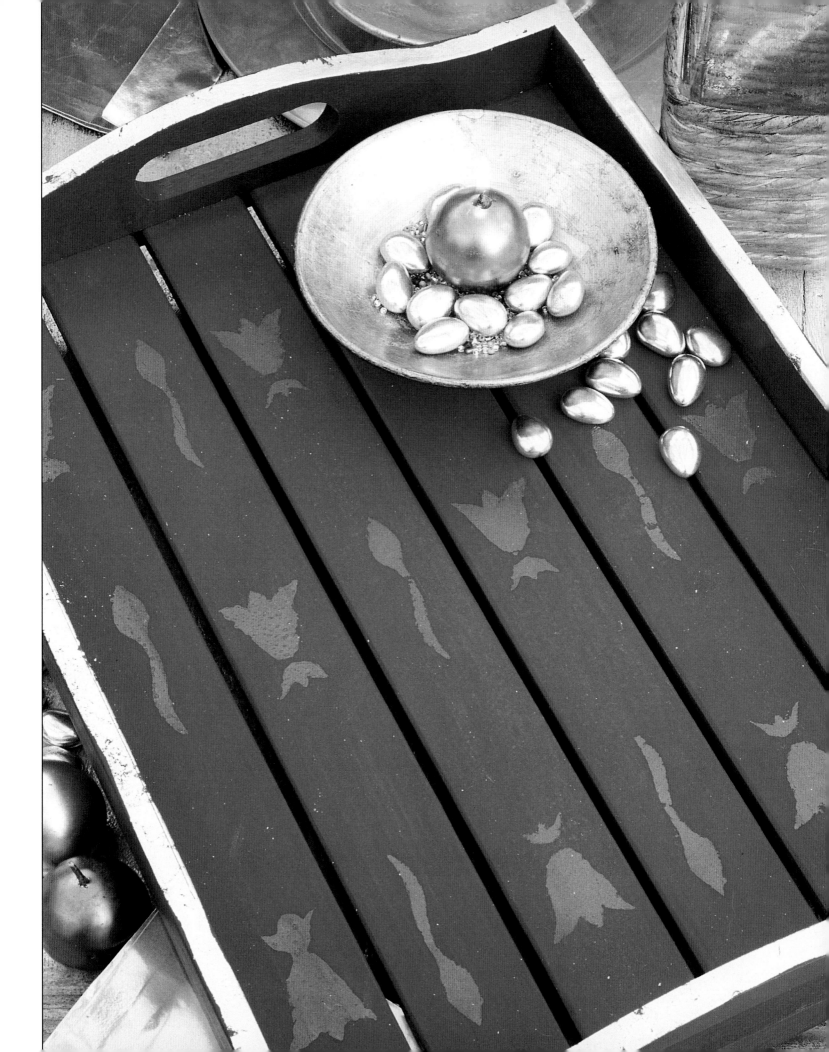

Icon Painting

It might seem rather a daunting project to make your own icon, but with care (and a little cheating), you can reproduce a beautiful medieval-style painting. Gilding is used to add antique authenticity and the deep red tones of the painting match those of Italian religious frescoes. This technique can be used for the image of your choice

YOU WILL NEED

small piece of plain wood or
   fiberboard
chisel
sandpaper
acrylic wood primer
1-inch paintbrush
reference for icon picture
tracing paper
pencil
assorted acrylic paints
paint pan
red acrylic gesso

assorted acrylic bristle brushes
artist's palette
water-based size
gold Dutch metal leaf
burnishing brush or soft cloth
steel wool
methylated spirit
amber shellac varnish
amber French enamel varnish
blackboard paint
quick-drying clear matte acrylic
   varnish

1 Use a chisel to roughen the edges of the wood or fiberboard and sand down. Paint with acrylic primer and leave to dry for 1 to 2 hours.

2 Trace or copy the basic icon design from a reference book or other source, or devise your own design.

3 Transfer the tracing to the wood and fill in the details of the design freehand with a pencil.

4 Dilute some acrylic paint for the background with a little water. Fill in the background with an acrylic bristle brush.

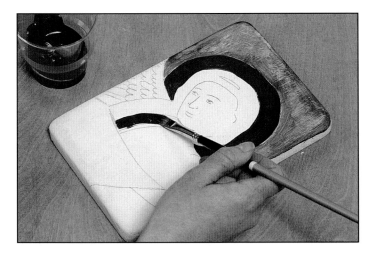

5 Leave the background to dry. Paint the halo and sleeve band in red acrylic gesso and leave to dry for 30 to 40 minutes.

6 Finish the painting, keeping the colors pale and as close to those of the original as possible to give the illusion of age. Leave to dry thoroughly.

7 Paint a thin, even coat of water-based size onto the halo and sleeve band and leave for 20 to 30 minutes, until the size becomes clear and tacky. ➤

8 Gild the halo and sleeve band using gold Dutch metal leaf. Burnish with a burnishing brush or soft cloth to remove the excess leaf and to add luster. Dip some steel wool into a little methylated spirit and gently rub the gilded areas to reveal some of the base coat.

9 Paint a thin, even coat of amber shellac onto the gilded areas and leave to dry for 30 minutes to 1 hour. Using French enamel varnish, paint the halo and sleeve band. Leave to dry for 30 minutes. Use blackboard paint to add details.

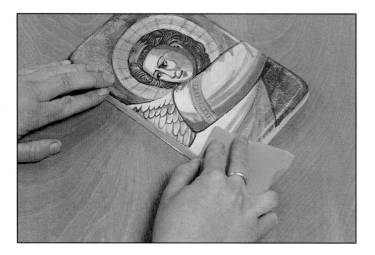

10 When completely dry, lightly sand the rest of the painting to distress it. Do not rub too hard.

11 Paint the edges of the wooden block in blackboard paint and leave to dry for 3 to 4 hours.

12 Seal the entire painting and the sides with quick-drying matte transparent varnish and leave to dry for 3 to 4 hours.

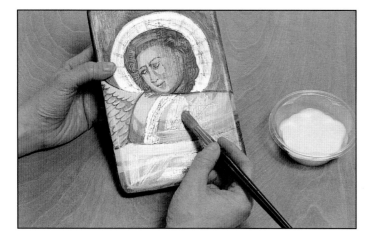

Napkin Rings

These napkin rings will add a touch of theatrical glamour to your dining table. They started life as plastic piping and were embellished cheaply using Dutch metal leaf and plastic jewels to create deceptively expensive-looking accessories from virtually nothing. Look out for interesting beads and other decorative items for further embellishments. Bead shops and haberdashers are often a good source ∾

YOU WILL NEED

plastic piping

black marker pen

coping saw

sandpaper

red oxide spray primer

water-based size

1-inch paintbrushes

gold Dutch metal leaf

burnishing brush or soft cloth

amber shellac varnish

dome-shaped jewels

glue gun and glue sticks

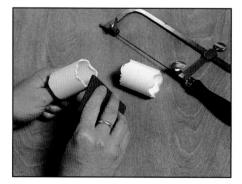

1 Mark off equal sections of plastic piping and cut with a coping saw. Sand down the edges until smooth.

2 Spray with red oxide spray primer and leave to dry.

3 Paint on a thin, even coat of water-based size and leave for 20 to 30 minutes, until it becomes clear and tacky.

4 Carefully lay the gold Dutch metal leaf onto the surface to cover the whole area. Burnish with a burnishing brush or soft cloth to remove the excess leaf and bring up the luster.

5 Seal with a thin, even coat of amber shellac varnish and leave to dry for 45 minutes to 1 hour.

6 Glue dome-shaped jewels around the center of the napkin rings using a glue gun.

CHERUB BOX

As the trend for paint effects gains momentum,

unpainted fiberboard forms are becoming more

readily available and can be found in many outlets.

This small hinged box has a classic look, which is

enhanced by gilding. It is given a baroque appearance

by the addition of the cherub

YOU WILL NEED

small wooden box with hinge
glue gun and glue sticks
cherub Christmas decoration
red oxide paint
1-inch paintbrushes
water-based size
gold Dutch metal leaf
burnishing brush or soft cloth
steel wool
methylated spirit

amber shellac varnish
pink acrylic paint
paint pan
soft cloth

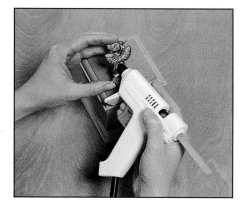

1 Use a glue gun to stick the cherub at an angle to the top of the box. Leave to dry for 10 minutes.

2 Prime the box with red oxide paint and leave to dry for 1 to 2 hours.

3 Paint on a thin, even coat of water-based size and leave for 20 to 30 minutes, until it becomes clear and tacky.

4 Gild the surface with gold Dutch metal leaf, ensuring that the whole area is covered. Burnish with a burnishing brush or soft cloth to remove the excess leaf and bring up the luster.

5 Dip some steel wool into a little methylated spirit and gently rub to reveal some of the base coat. Seal with a thin, even coat of amber shellac and leave to dry for 30 minutes to 1 hour.

6 Mix some pink acrylic paint with water and paint over the surface. Rub off most of the paint with a cloth, leaving only a little paint in the details. Leave to dry for 30 minutes.

MEDIEVAL CLOCK

This amazing medieval-style clock started life as a plastic office wall clock

that was found broken and discarded. By adding fiberboard and using simple

techniques, including gilding, of course, the clock was given an astounding

transformation to make it a stunning addition to any interior

YOU WILL NEED

old school or office wall clock

sandpaper

3/4-inch fiberboard, 32 x 32 inches

magic marker

jigsaw

pair of compasses (or string and pen)

general-purpose sealant and gun

cardboard

craft knife

wood glue

nails

hammer

artist's palette

petroleum jelly

filler

filling knife

1-inch paintbrushes

white acrylic primer

red latex paint

water-based size

Dutch metal leaf in aluminum, gold
  and copper

burnishing brush or soft cloth

amber shellac varnish

water-based varnishing wax

soft cloths

acrylic paints in purple and green

paint pan

1/12-inch thick cardboard

drill

clock movement

red oxide spray primer

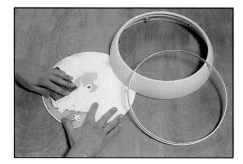

1 Dismantle the clock, removing the old movement, hands and glass. Wash the remaining parts of the clock in hot soapy water. Sand down the clockface and surround with sandpaper and reassemble the basic clock.

2 Trace the template from the back of the book. Transfer onto the fiberboard with the magic marker, using the clock surround as a guide for scaling up the shape.

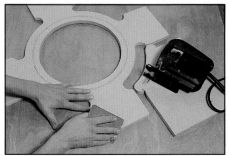

3 Using a jigsaw fitted with a narrow blade, cut out the shape. Cut out a circle in the center slightly smaller than the clock surround to allow access to the back of the clock. Sand down all the edges.

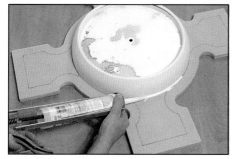

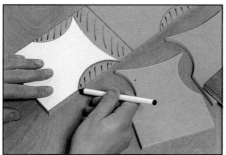

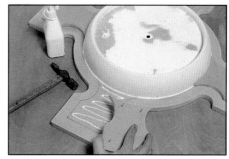

4 Using a general-purpose sealant gun, glue the clock surround onto the fiberboard, applying thick beading to the outside edge and a larger amount of sealant to the inside edge at the back. Leave the structure to dry for at least 24 hours.

5 Make a cardboard template of the raised areas of the cross. Cut a piece of fiberboard to the same width as the template, then draw around the template four times on to the fiberboard. Cut out the pieces with the jigsaw and sand the edges.

6 Using a craft knife, shave off the bottom of the edge of each piece where it will meet the line of sealant around the clock surround. Fix with wood glue and nail the pieces in position.   ➤

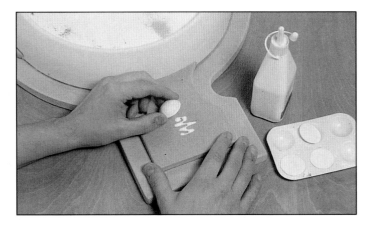

7 Grease a small artist's palette with petroleum jelly and fill four compartments with filler. Leave to dry and pop from the mold. Stick one half-sphere in the center of each raised piece.

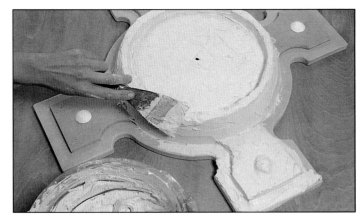

8 Mix the filler into a thick paste and use a filling knife to spread it over the entire clock. Try to maintain an even thickness of approximately ⅛ inch all over.

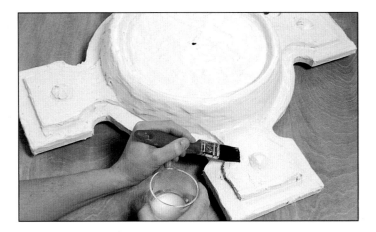

9 Dip a 1-inch paintbrush in water and smooth the surface using a stroking action always in the same direction. Work your way around the clock two or three times.

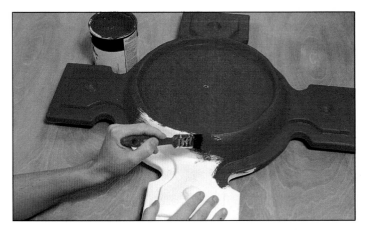

10 When the filler is completely dry, lightly sand the high parts and any rough edges. Paint on a coat of acrylic primer and leave to dry for 1 to 2 hours. Paint on a coat of red latex and leave to dry for 2 to 3 hours.

11 Apply water-based size to the areas you wish to gild in aluminum. Leave the size for 20 to 30 minutes. Gild with aluminum and burnish. Gild the gold areas with gold Dutch metal leaf in the same way.

12 Seal the gold areas with two coats of amber shellac varnish and the aluminum areas with water-based varnishing wax. Leave the wax to dry, then buff with a soft cloth.

13 Mix some purple acrylic paint with a little water and paint over the clock. Leave to set for 5 minutes, then rub off most of the paint with a cloth, leaving only a little paint in areas of detail.

14 Trace the hands from the back of the book onto plastic or cardboard and cut out. Drill two holes slightly larger than the holes in the hands supplied with the clock movement.

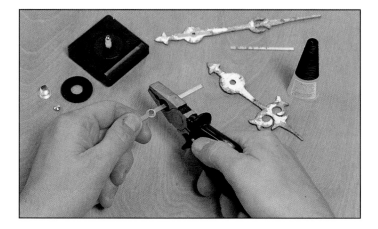

15 Snip the supplied hands to fit the new hands and glue to the back of the new hands.

16 Spray the hands with red oxide spray primer and leave to dry for 1 hour. Size the hands and leave for 20 to 30 minutes, until the size is clear and tacky. Gild with crumpled copper Dutch metal leaf.

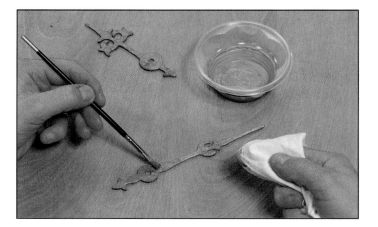

17 Roughly dab some green acrylic paint onto the hands using random brush strokes. Using a damp cloth, dab on more paint to build up the crusty effect.

18 Following the manufacturer's instructions, fit the new movement to the clock face and fit the hands. Add a dab of paint to the fixing nut to finish.

HARVEST POD BOX

This lovely gilded box frame, with its woodwashed interior, is used to display an arrangement of gilded pods, roots and fruits in a celebration of autumnal bounty. The box is quite simple to make and you can have the glass cut to size at the shop if you prefer not to do it yourself. This project shows how gilding can highlight the texture and shapes of natural objects beautifully

YOU WILL NEED

length of pine, $2^{1}/_{2}$ x $^{1}/_{4}$ inch

ruler

pencil

saw

miter saw

$^{1}/_{2}$-inch panel pins

hammer

length of tongue and groove pine

azure-blue matte latex paint

paint pan

1-inch bristle brushes

sandpaper

deep-recess hockey-stick framing

picture glass

glass-cutter (optional)

red oxide primer

water-based size

Dutch metal leaf in gold, copper
  and aluminum

burnishing brush or soft cloth

dried fruits and pods

amber shellac varnish

transparent acrylic varnish

white wax crayon

glue gun and glue sticks

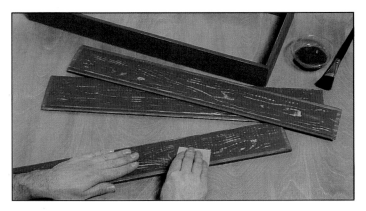

1 Cut the pine to the required lengths to build the sides of the box. Use a miter saw or make butt joints, whichever you prefer, and tack together with panel pins. Cut the tongue and groove pine to the required size to make a base for the box.

2 Thin down the latex paint and paint the sides of the box and the lengths of tongue and groove blue. Leave to dry for 30 minutes. Lightly sand the painted pieces to create an aged effect. Tack the tongue and groove pine to the sides with panel pins.

3 To make the frame, measure and cut the hockey-stick framing using a miter saw, so that it easily slides over the sides of the box.

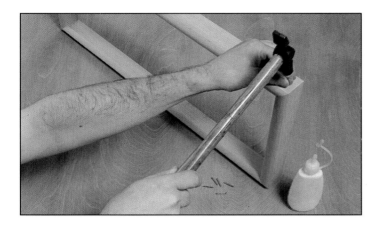

4 Tack the frame together with panel pins.

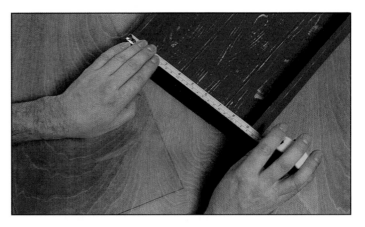

5 Measure and cut the glass (or have it cut) to fit inside the frame.

6 Paint the frame with red oxide primer and leave to dry for 2 to 3 hours. Paint on a thin, even coat of water-based size and leave for 20 to 30 minutes, until it becomes clear and tacky. Gild with gold Dutch metal leaf, crushing the leaf as you go along to create a broken effect. Burnish with a burnishing brush or soft cloth to remove the excess leaf.

7 Paint the fruits and pods with red oxide primer and leave to dry. Paint on water-based size and leave for 20 to 30 minutes, until it becomes clear and tacky. Gild some of the pods and fruits with copper Dutch metal leaf, some with gold and some with aluminum, crushing the leaf as before. Burnish with a burnishing brush or soft cloth.

8 Seal the gold frame and gold pods and fruits with amber shellac varnish and leave to dry for 45 minutes to 1 hour.

9 Seal the aluminum and copper pods and fruits with transparent acrylic varnish and leave to dry for 1 to 2 hours. ➤

10 Arrange the pods and fruits in rows on the base of the box and mark their positions with a white wax crayon. Use the glue gun to glue them in place and leave to dry.

11 Fit the glass over the pods and slide the gold frame into place.

12 Secure the frame to the box with panel pins.

HEART BROOCH AND HAT PIN

This little brooch is made from fiberboard and gilded using a distressed technique. The delicate pin will make the perfect finish to a wedding hat. It is made from modeling clay, gilded and decorated with jewels

YOU WILL NEED

piece of fiberboard, 4 x 4 inches

black magic marker

coping saw

sandpaper or chisel

pale blue spray paint

water-based size

two bristle brushes

gold Dutch metal leaf

burnishing brush or soft cloth

steel wool

methylated spirit

acrylic varnishing wax

soft cloth

glue gun and glue sticks

brooch back

hat pin and cap

modeling clay

rolling pin

modeling tools

gilt cream

soft cloth

plastic jewels

HEART BROOCH

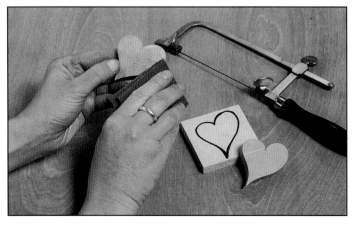

1 Draw a heart shape on the fiberboard in black magic marker and cut out with a coping saw. With sandpaper or a chisel, roughen the edges to add texture.

2 Spray both sides of the heart with pale blue spray paint and leave to dry. Paint a thin, even coat of water-based size onto the front of the heart and leave for 20 to 30 minutes, until it becomes clear and tacky.

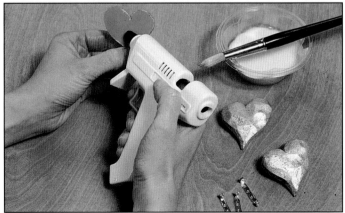

3 Cover the entire sized area with gold Dutch metal leaf. Remove the excess leaf with a burnishing brush or soft cloth. Gently distress the surface using steel wool and a little methylated spirit.

4 Seal with acrylic varnishing wax and leave to dry. Buff with a soft cloth. Glue a brooch back onto the back of the heart. ➤

HEART HAT PIN

1 Warm and roll out the modeling clay to a thickness of about 1/4 inch. Cut out a heart shape and round off the edges. Use modeling tools to make patterns and indentations in the clay.

2 Insert the hat pin into the base of the heart to a depth of about 1 inch. Enlarge the hole slightly by circling the pin, then remove the pin. Bake the heart in the oven following the manufacturer's instructions and leave to cool.

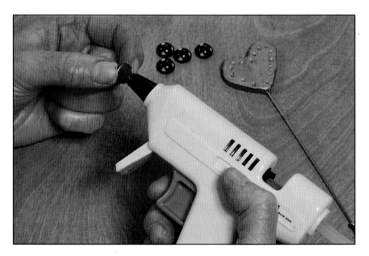

3 Rub gilt cream into both sides of the heart and leave to dry. Buff with a soft cloth.

4 Glue the hat pin into the base of the heart and glue plastic jewels onto the heart.

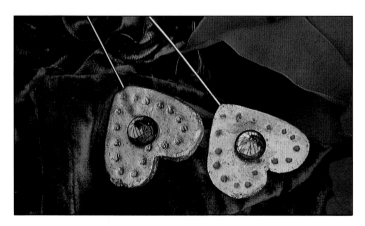

Left: Make a series of hat pins to give as gifts.

STAR COOKIES AND COASTERS

Stars have always been a source of wonder and fascination. There are many different star shapes, so experiment with your own designs. Gilded stars make beautiful ornaments and, although they are mostly associated with Christmas, there is no reason why stars shouldn't decorate your home at any time of the year ∽

YOU WILL NEED

scissors
24-carat edible gold leaf
thin cardboard
fine paintbrush
piping gel
cookies, bought or homemade
stencil brush
squares of fiberboard
black magic marker
coping saw
sandpaper
dark blue spray paint
water-based size
1-inch paintbrushes
gold Dutch metal leaf
burnishing brush or soft cloth
steel wool
methylated spirit
amber shellac varnish
sticky-backed felt

STAR COOKIES

1 Cut out star shapes from the edible leaf. Don't over handle the gold leaf, or you will spoil the shine.

2 Make a star-shaped stencil from thin cardboard. Use a fine paintbrush to paint piping gel through the shape onto each cookie.

3 Lay the gold stars paper side up on the piping gel, using the stencil as a guide. Press down firmly with a stencil brush and gently peel away the backing paper. Leave to harden for 24 hours. ➤

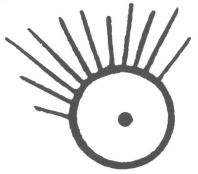

STAR COASTERS

1 Draw the star shape on the fiberboard and cut out with a coping saw. Round off the edges with sandpaper.

2 Prime the star on both sides with dark blue spray paint and leave to dry. Paint a coat of water-based size on both sides of the star and leave for 20 to 30 minutes, until it becomes clear and tacky.

3 Gild both sides of the star with gold Dutch metal leaf, covering the whole area. Burnish with a burnishing brush or soft cloth to remove the excess leaf. Dip some steel wool into a little methylated spirit and gently distress the edges of the star.

4 Seal on both sides with a thin, even coat of amber shellac varnish and leave to dry for 45 minutes to an hour. Cut out a star shape from sticky-backed felt, peel off the backing paper and carefully stick to one side of the star.

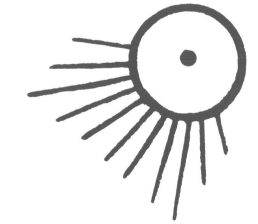

Left: The finished coasters can be used as a base for candles.

GILDED FRIVOLITIES

Let your imagination run wild, and consider gilding all kinds of items, from pinecones and pebbles to your very own gilded birdcage! Any item, no matter how unassuming, will benefit from a touch of gold.

GILDING THE LILY

Now that you are familiar with the techniques and possibilities of gilding, the fun really starts!

You can gild virtually anything, from shells and nuts, to a whole meal. Gilding is the ultimate way to make your mark on all manner of objects for the home, and not just for celebrations or special festivities, but all year long. Gilding food is the last word in decadence, and has been practiced by the Indian nobility for centuries – astound your dinner guests by indulging in the Midas touch. Traditionalists might shudder at the idea of gilding nuts and shells, but, like many natural materials, the textures provide a wonderful surface to work on, and with the fantastic array of reasonably priced composite leaf on offer, projects such as

Above: This astrological clockface is enhanced with gold Dutch metal leaf.

these are not nearly as costly as it might appear. Old pieces of driftwood are also worth salvaging from walks on the beach; their wonderful gnarled appearance can be further embellished with composite leaf, to create a striking contemporary piece of beauty.

Gilded items make exquisite gifts that will be treasured by the recipient for years to come, transforming the mundane into something truly spectacular. You needn't restrict yourself to gold tones, either; composite leaf exists in almost any metallic shade, so let your imagination run riot, and look out for interesting shapes and textures to create unique objects that are every bit as beautiful – and covetable – as more traditional pieces.

Left: Decorative plaster shells are embellished with gold and silver leaf.

Right: Silver metallic powder was used sparingly, but to great effect, on this polymer clay frame.

GILDED BIRDCAGE

Now you can have your own bird in a gilded cage! This

pretty, old-fashioned birdcage was found in a junk

shop. A rusted gilt technique is used here, since it is an

easier way of gilding awkwardly shaped objects. Filling

the many nooks and crannies with broken leaf ensures

that as much of the cage as possible is covered ⌒

YOU WILL NEED

birdcage

red oxide spray primer

water-based size

1-inch paintbrushes

old sheet (optional)

broken gold Dutch metal leaf
 (schlag)

dish

soft-bristled brush

water-based clear matte varnish

powder pigment in burnt umber
 and yellow-ochre

paint pans

soft cloth (optional)

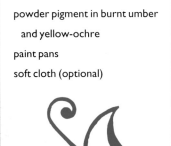

1 Spray an even coat of red oxide spray primer over the birdcage inside and out. Using spray primer makes covering the whole cage much easier than using a paintbrush and ensures an even coverage.

2 Paint water-based size onto the cage, making sure the whole cage is covered inside and out. Access the interior through the cage door. Leave the size for about 20 to 30 minutes, until it becomes tacky and clear. ➤

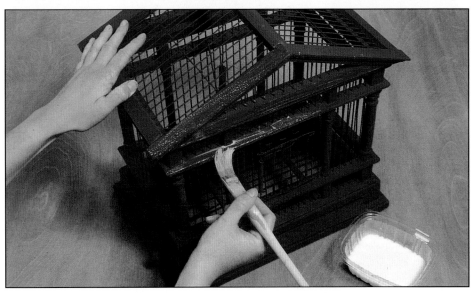

3 Place the cage on a sheet, if desired, to collect any of the broken leaf. Pour the leaf in a dish and sprinkle the leaf onto the cage.

4 Resize any patchy areas and use the excess leaf caught in the sheet or on the work surface to fill them in.

5 Burnish the cage with a soft brush until all the loose leaf has been removed and the surface is as smooth as possible.

6 Pour some water-based varnish into two saucers or paint pans and add burnt umber pigment to one and yellow-ochre pigment to the other.

7 Using a separate brush for each color, dab on patches of the two colors to build up the rust effect. Try not to make the dabs too heavy and make sure that some of the leaf is still visible underneath. Wipe gently with a cloth if necessary.

8 Continue until the whole surface is covered and leave to dry for 1 to 2 hours. The varnish will seal the surface, so there is no need for further sealing.

STAR TREE DECORATIONS

These simple tree ornaments are easy to make from fiberboard using a coping saw. Gilded using a distressed technique and embellished with a single bead and ribbon, they make long-lasting and individual decorations. Hang them individually from a Christmas tree, or in groups on lengths of different ribbons

YOU WILL NEED

squares of fiberboard, 6 x 6 inches

black magic marker

coping saw or fretsaw

sandpaper

electric or hand drill

red oxide spray primer

water-based size

1-inch bristle brushes

Dutch metal leaf in gold and aluminum

burnishing brush or soft cloth

steel wool

methylated spirit

shellac varnish

acrylic varnishing wax

acrylic paints in green and blue

paint pans

soft cloths

glue gun and glue sticks

dome-shaped plastic jewels

lengths of ribbon

1 Trace the template from the back of the book. Draw the star shape onto the fiberboard using a black magic marker.

2 Using a coping saw or fretsaw, carefully cut out the shape. Sand down any rough edges and smooth the corners. ➤

133

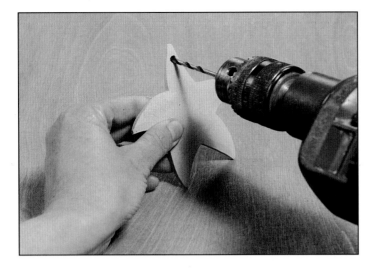

3 Mark a dot just in from the end of one point. Drill a hole with an electric or hand drill.

4 Spray both sides of the star with red oxide spray primer and leave to dry.

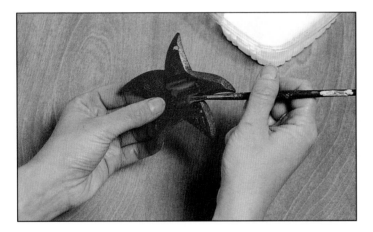

5 Paint on a thin, even coat of water-based size and leave for 20 to 30 minutes, until it becomes clear and tacky.

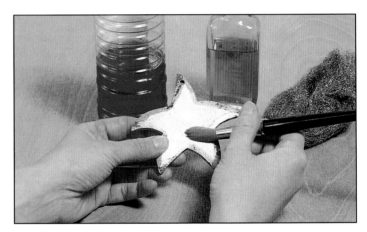

6 Gild some stars with gold and some with aluminum Dutch metal leaf. Burnish with a burnishing brush or soft cloth. Dip some steel wool into a little methylated spirit and gently distress the edges of each star. Paint an even coat of shellac varnish onto the gold leaf and acrylic varnishing wax onto the aluminum leaf.

7 In separate containers, mix some green and blue acrylic paint with a little water. Paint the gold stars green and the aluminum stars blue. Leave to set for 5 minutes, then remove most of the paint with a cloth. Dampen the cloth if the paint has set too much. Stick a dome-shaped jewel into the center of each star and tie a ribbon through each hole for hanging.

GILDED NUTS

Nuts are ideal subjects for gilding as they have so much texture and detail and they can be put to all sorts of decorative uses. They would make a sumptuous table decoration for a party or look lovely attached to gift boxes or in a bowl at Christmas

YOU WILL NEED

assorted nuts
red oxide spray primer
water-based size
1/2-inch paintbrushes
gold Dutch metal leaf
burnishing brush or soft cloth
amber shellac varnish

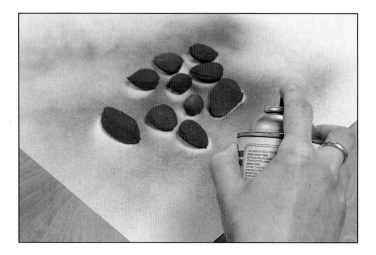

1 Spray the nuts with red oxide spray primer and leave to dry for 30 minutes to 1 hour.

2 Paint on a thin, even coat of water-based size and leave for 20 to 30 minutes, until it becomes clear and tacky.

3 Wrap the sized nuts in sheets of gold Dutch metal leaf, making sure that they are completely covered and that no recesses or details are exposed.

4 Burnish with a burnishing brush or soft cloth to remove the excess leaf. Seal with a thin, even coat of amber shellac varnish and leave to dry for 30 minutes to 1 hour.

WOODEN BEAD NECKLACE

Simple wooden balls available from craft shops are transformed by gilding to make a glittering necklace. Experiment with leaf or powders in different colors and alternate the colors of the beads on the string for stunningly original jewelry. This necklace could also be used as an unusual tie-back

YOU WILL NEED

assorted wooden balls

vise

drill and fine bit

hammer

small nails

wood off-cut

red oxide spray primer

water-based size

1-inch paintbrushes

Dutch metal leaf in gold, copper and aluminum

burnishing brush or soft cloth

amber shellac varnish

acrylic varnishing wax

soft cloth

scissors

leather thongs

1 Holding each ball in turn in a vise, drill a hole through the center.

2 Hammer small nails into the off-cut of wood to make a rack. Place the balls on the nails and spray with red oxide primer. Leave to dry thoroughly.

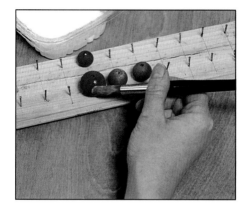

3 Paint a thin, even coat of water-based size onto the balls and leave for 20 to 30 minutes, until the size becomes clear and tacky.

4 Gild the balls in different colors of Dutch metal leaf and burnish with a burnishing brush or soft cloth to remove the excess leaf.

5 Seal the gold balls with amber shellac varnish and the copper and aluminum balls with acrylic varnishing wax. Buff the wax with a soft cloth after 1 to 2 hours to bring up the luster.

6 Cut lengths of leather thong and thread the balls onto it, alternating each color. Tie the ends of the thong in a knot.

GILDED STONES

The texture and detail on stones make them ideal candidates for gilding. They would make a pretty edging for a path in a small garden or surprising decorations for a rock garden or border. As interior decorations, they can be arranged in a conservatory or garden room, or clustered around plant pots

YOU WILL NEED

selection of stones and pebbles

white acrylic primer

1-inch paintbrush

water-based size

Dutch metal leaf in gold,
    aluminum and copper

burnishing brush or soft cloth

acrylic varnishing wax

soft cloth

1 Remove any earth or grit from the stones, then wash them well and leave to dry. Paint with white acrylic primer and leave to dry for 1 to 2 hours.

2 Paint each stone with a thin coat of water-based size and leave for 20 to 30 minutes, until it becomes clear and tacky.

3 Lay the Dutch metal onto the surface, one sheet at a time, to cover the whole area, so that you have several stones in each color. Burnish with a burnishing brush or cloth to remove the excess leaf.

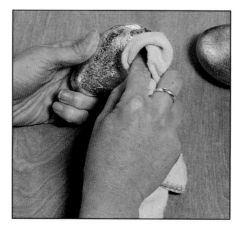

4 Seal each stone with a thin coat of acrylic varnishing wax. Leave to dry for 1 to 2 hours.

5 Buff with a soft cloth to bring up the luster of the leaf.

CHAPLET

Dating back to Roman times, a chaplet is a wreath of leaves, gold and gems that was worn on the head on ceremonial occasions. This simple chaplet made from real laurel leaves is constructed using florist's wire and tape and is then sprayed gold for the imperial Roman touch

YOU WILL NEED

laurel branch, with approximately
  66 small, fresh leaves
florist's wire
wire cutters
florist's tape
scissors
gold spray paint

1 Gently pluck the leaves from the laurel, leaving a small stalk. If necessary, cut the florist's wire into 6 inch lengths.

2 To single-leg mount the leaves, thread a wire through the leaf about 1 inch from the stalk. Twist the wire ends together to make a branch.

3 Bind the stalks together with florist's tape, overlapping the leaves in pairs to make the two sides of the wreath.

4 At the top end of each side of the wreath, make a hook in the wires. Hook the two sides together to make a circular shape, with the leaves pointing toward the front.

5 Using florist's tape, attach more leaves at the base of the wreath to form a bow shape.

6 Spray a fine mist of gold spray paint over the wreath, holding the can 12 inches away from the wreath and passing over several times to give an even coverage. Leave to dry for 30 to 40 minutes.

PINECONES

The naturally intricate shape of pinecones looks wonderful when highlighted by the addition of gold spray and glitter. They could be arranged in a gilded bowl, to make a striking table decoration. They could also be arranged in a garland or wired individually and hung from a tree at Christmastime

YOU WILL NEED

pinecones

red oxide spray primer

gold and silver sprays

glue gun and glue sticks

assorted glitters

saucer

1 To provide a good base color for the gold spray, prime the cones with red oxide spray primer and leave to dry. Ensure all the recesses and details are well covered.

2 Spray the cones several times with gold or silver spray, so that you have several cones in different colors. Hold the can 10 to 12 inches away from the cones as you spray. Leave to dry.

3 Heat up the glue gun and apply a little glue to the tips of each cone. Be careful not to apply too much.

4 Working quickly, sprinkle the glitter onto the cones so that it sticks to the glued tips. Use a saucer to catch the excess glitter.

DRIFTWOOD

The twisted shapes of driftwood weathered by the elements make wonderful bases for gilding projects. Use the finished piece as an indoor or outdoor decoration at any time of year. Dutch metal transforms a naturally mysterious object into one of intriguing splendor ❧

YOU WILL NEED

driftwood

green spray paint

water-based size

2-inch paintbrushes

aluminum Dutch metal leaf

burnishing brush or soft cloth

water-based varnishing wax

soft cloth

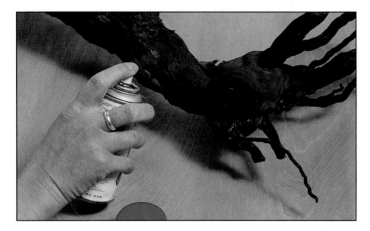

1 Make sure that the wood is dry and remove any loose bits of wood or dirt. Spray the entire surface with green spray paint and leave to dry for at least 1 hour.

2 Paint on the water-based size, covering as much of the surface as possible. Leave for about 20 to 30 minutes, until the size becomes clear and tacky.

3 Gild the wood with aluminum leaf and burnish with a burnishing brush or soft cloth to remove the excess leaf.

4 Paint an even coat of varnishing wax over the surface. Leave to dry for 1 hour, then buff with a soft cloth.

CHRISTMAS GARLAND

Christmas is the obvious time of year for using gilding to decorate the home. The allure of shimmering metallic finishes adds to the magic of the season. This garland is made from dried flowers and other ornaments, sprayed gold and built up around a chicken wire tube. Collect a variety of objects, and experiment with different shapes and textures

YOU WILL NEED

florist's wire

wire cutters

ruler

dried flowers, seedheads,
  pods, leaves and grasses

fresh ginger

pinecones

gold spray paint in three
  shades

chicken wire

sphagnum moss

cherub decorations

satin roses

paper bows

2 yards cord

1 Cut the florist's wire into 8-inch lengths. Wrap the end of each natural item with a piece of wire, leaving 4½ inches of wire protruding. Leaves and grasses may be bound together in bunches.

2 Hold each piece by the end of the wire and spray with gold paint, so that you have several pieces in each of the three shades. Leave to dry for 30 minutes.

3 Cut a piece of chicken wire 6 inches wide and as long as required. Curl up the edges and fill with moss. The moss will hold the gilded pieces, so make sure it is packed evenly.

4 Join the edges of the chicken wire together around the moss to make a tube. Pinch the edges of wire together to close the tube. Any stubborn gaps may be closed with florist's wire.

5 Push the wire ends of the gilded pieces through the chicken wire and into the moss, bending back the wire as you insert it for added security.

6 Continue to build up the garland, adding the cherub decorations, satin roses and paper bows to the gilded pieces to achieve the desired effect. Tie a length of cord to each end of the garland for hanging.

GILDED INDIAN MEAL

The Mogul Emperor who built the

beautiful Taj Mahal used to hold all-white banquets

within the Agra fort on nights with a full moon.

Everything was white and silver, including the food.

The leaf used here is perfectly edible

YOU WILL NEED

scissors

edible silver leaf (warq)

tweezers

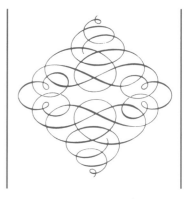

WHITE CHICKEN KORMA (Safed Murgh Korma – Agra)

TO SERVE FOUR:

1½ tsp poppy seeds	2 cinnamon sticks or bay leaves
2 oz blanched almonds	1 clove
2 oz unsalted cashew nuts	2¼ lb boneless chicken breasts
3 chopped green chilies	½ tsp ground nutmeg
2 tsp chopped garlic	½ tsp ground mace
2 tsp ground ginger	1¼ cups heavy cream
12 oz chopped onions	
⅓ cup ghee (clarified butter)	
4 green cardamom pods	

Heat a frying pan without any liquid and dry-roast the first seven ingredients. Cool, then grind to a fine paste.

Heat the ghee in a frying pan. Fry the cardamom, cinnamon and clove until the clove swells. Add the chicken and heat until it has released all its juices and is almost dry. Add the nutmeg, mace and prepared paste.

Stir in the cream.

1 Place the chicken korma on individual plates. Cut moon shapes from the edible leaf, carefully avoiding too much contact with the leaf, since this will dull the shine.

2 Using tweezers, gently place several moon shapes on top of the chicken korma. Serve with rice, garnishes and other accompaniments of your choice.

TEMPLATES

To enlarge templates to the size required, you can either use a photocopier, or a grid system.

For the grid system, trace the template from the book on to tracing paper, and draw a grid of evenly spaced squares over your tracing. To scale up, draw a larger grid on to another piece of paper. Copy the outline on to the second grid by taking each square individually and drawing the relevant part of the outline in the larger square. Finally, draw over the lines to make sure they are continuous.

STAR DECORATIONS

STAR COASTERS

HEART CUSHION

STAR CUSHION

TILES

LAMPSHADE

VASE

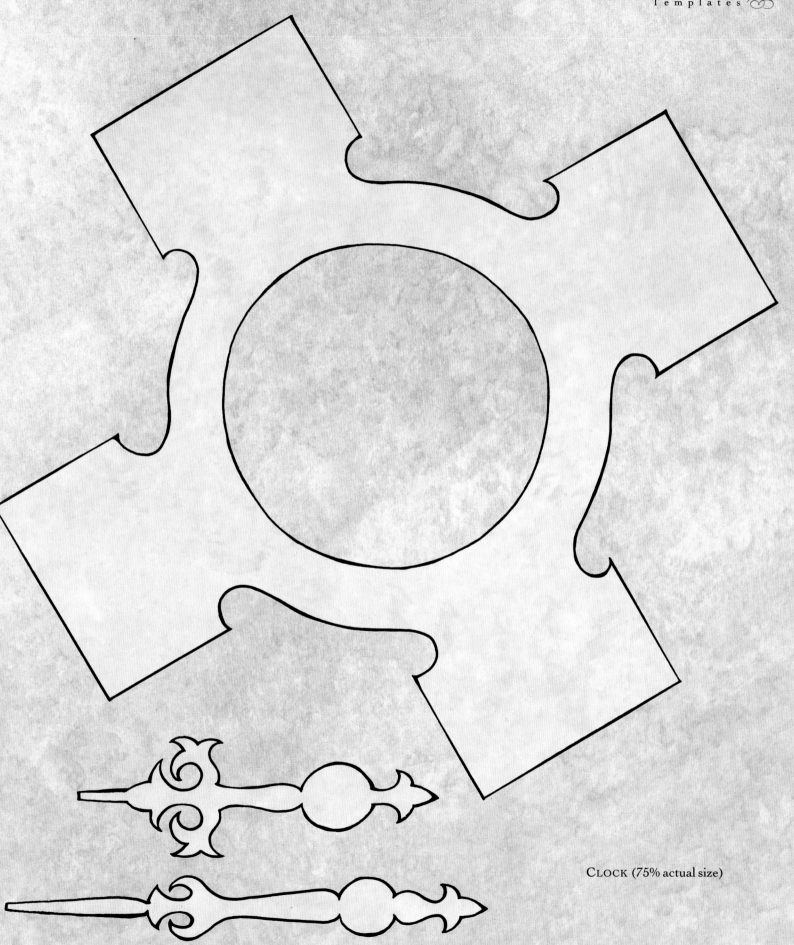

CLOCK (75% actual size)

Suppliers

Architectural Sculpture and Restoration
242 Lafayette Street
New York, NY 10012
(212) 431-5873
Ornamental plaster

Art Essentials of New York
3 Cross Street
Suffern, NY 10901
(800) 283-5323
Gilding supplies

Creative Craft House
P.O. Box 2567
Bullhead City, AZ 86430
(520) 754-3300
General craft supplies

The Durham Company
54 Woodland Street
Newburyport, MA 01950
(508) 465-3493
Gilding supplies

Esoteric Sign Supply
1644 Wilmington Boulevard
Wilmington, California 90744
(310) 549-6622
Gilding supplies

Frog Tool Company, Ltd.
2169 Illinois Route 26
Dixon, IL 61021
(815) 288-3811, (800) 648-1220
Hand woodworking tools and finishing materials

Gold Leaf & Metallic Powders, Inc.
74 Trinity Place, Suite 1200
New York, NY 10006
(212) 267-4900, (800) 322-0323
Gilding supplies

Geiger's
P.O. Box 73070
Pasadena, CA 91109
(800) 423-4181
Jewelry supplies

Klockit
P.O. Box 636
Lake Geneva, WI 53147
(414) 248-7000, (800) 556-2548
Clock parts

Knossos
538 Avenue of the Americas
New York, NY 10011
(212) 242-0966
Particleboard furniture

Pearl Discount Art & Craft
3756 Roswell Road
Atlanta, GA 30342
(404) 233-9400
Paint and gilding supplies

Pearl Paint Co.
308 Canal Street
New York, NY 10013
(212) 431-7932, (800) 221-6845
Paint and gilding supplies

Sculpture House Casting
155 West 26th Street
New York, NY 10001
(212) 645-9430
Ornamental plaster

Sinopia
229 Valencia Street
San Francisco, CA 94103
(415) 621-2898
Gilding supplies

Star Scenic Supply
621 Brookhaven Drive
Orlando, FL 32803
(407) 895-3944
Gilding supplies

Stu-Art Supplies
2045 Grand Avenue
Baldwin, NY 11510
(516) 546-5151
Raw picture frames

**Utrecht Art & Drafting
Supplies**
111 Fourth Avenue
New York, NY 10003
(212) 777-5353, (800) 352-9016

$\mathscr{I}$NDEX

BIBLIOGRAPHY

The Gilder's Manual, The Society of Gilders, Excelsior Publishing House, New York.

Practical Gilding, by Peter and Anne McTaggart, Mac & Me Ltd, 1984.

Sign Work: A Craftsman's Manual, by Bill Stewart, Collins BSP, London, 1984.

Formulas for Artists, by Robert Massey, Batsford, London, 1968.

The Craftsman's Handbook, by Andrea Cennini, New York, 1960.

The Romantic Interior: The British Collector at Home 1750–1850, by Clive Wainwright, Yale University Press, 1989.

Recipes for Surfaces, by Mindy Drucker and Pierre Finkelstein, Cassell, London, 1993.

Country Living Book of Paint Recipes, by Liz Wagstaff, Quadrille, London, 1995.

PICTURE CREDITS

The author and publishers would like to thank the following for the use of pictures reproduced in this book:

Bridgeman Art Library/Smithsonian Institution, Washington: p. 39 bottom

Lilli Curtiss: p. 12 bottom left and top, p. 13 bottom right

John Freeman: p. 10 bottom left and bottom right, p. 11, p. 38, p. 39 top

AUTHOR'S ACKNOWLEDGMENTS

My love and thanks to Mark for all his help and patience and to Netty for all her hard work, to Doug and Paul for their lovely pieces and to Clive and Jenny for the fun we had with the chaplet, to Lucy and Debbie for their wonderful work and a big thanks to my editors Lindsay and Joanna for their understanding and support, and to all at Anness and the many others who cannot be mentioned here.